Friends Under Construction

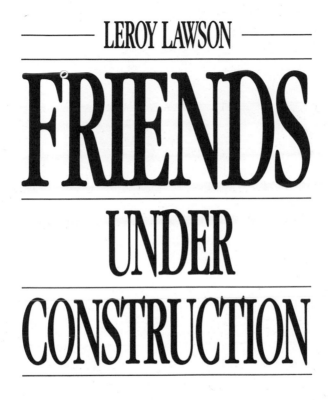

LEROY LAWSON

FRIENDS
UNDER
CONSTRUCTION

(s†u)® —— STANDARD PUBLISHING
Cincinnati, Ohio   11-39952

Unless otherwise noted, all Scripture quotations are from the *Holy Bible: New International Version,* © 1973, 1978, 1984 by the International Bible Society. Used by permission of Zondervan Bible Publishers and the International Bible Society.

Sharing the thoughts of his own heart, the author may express views not entirely consistent with those of the publisher.

Library of Congress Cataloging in Publication Data:

Lawson, E. LeRoy, 1938-
  Friends under construction/by E. LeRoy Lawson.
    p. cm.
  ISBN 0-87403-610-0
  1. Friendship—Religious aspects—Christianity. I. Title.
BV4647.F7L38 1990
241'.676—dc20   89-21732
                                                  CIP

CONTENTS

INTRODUCTION

"Spirituality" Is a Social Phenomenon
Philemon 1-3

We think about friendship all our lives. From the first tentative reaching out of the toddler to the tottering greetings of the oldest of cronies, every healthy human being seeks friends. Go back to Western Civilization's classic authors and you'll find Homer, Plato, and Xenophon praising the beauty of friendship; among Rome's intelligentsia, Cicero, Seneca, Horace, and Ovid, to name just a few, also studied its subtleties. Centuries later, Montaigne and Shakespeare added their compliments. But after them came the darkened minds of Nietzsche and Schopenhauer, wondering doubtfully whether friendship is even possible.

We don't use the word *friendship* in the church as often as it deserves. We prefer *fellowship;* it somehow sounds more religious. To listen to us, the uninitiated might conclude that friendship is something Christians reserve for life outside the church, while fellowship belongs inside. In truth, though, we enjoy a richer fellowship in church to the degree that we foster friendships there.

Leslie Weatherhead enhanced my understanding of the subject with his definition of the church: "Thus the church on earth began ... with men who were friends of Jesus, and in my opinion that ought still to be the test of membership."[1] Friends of Jesus. A motley crew they were, too, those first ones, and a motley crew they remain. Anyone seems acceptable in the church, even you and I (although we might, in an honest moment, be tempted to huff with Groucho Marx when he resigned from the Friars Club, "I don't want to belong to any club that would accept me as a member!")

This book is for every Christian who likes the idea of being one of the Friends of Jesus. Whether you are more comfortable with *fellowship* or *friendship* doesn't really matter, so long as you remember that a group's fellowship depends on its friendships. (*Friendship* implies reciprocity, love passing both ways between persons. *Fellowship,* although we should never allow the word to be so restricted, has grown institutional, more formal and structured.) In the following pages, we'll examine as many of the faces of friendship as time and space allow. At the end, we'll feel a little disappointed. The topic can't be telescoped into a book so small.

Whatever we say won't be enough; yet, in another sense, the word by itself says it all. Augustine Birrell called it something "the very sight of which in print makes the heart warm." On the other hand, we can't be blind to its flip side. Friendship isn't always an unmixed blessing. It was Voltaire, wasn't it, who grumbled, "God preserve me from my friends; I will take care of my enemies myself"? Jesus, who taught us more about friendship than anyone else and commanded us to love even our enemies, experienced no little trouble with His friends. ("Get thee behind me, Satan," He scolded His presumptuous friend Peter.) Obviously, the subject bears studying.

We can choose no better guide through the subject than Jesus, who taught, modeled, and commanded His disciples to befriend one another and the world. He hasn't changed His mind. He still expects His friends to follow His example (John 15:13). The Holy Spirit makes such love possible.

> For the Holy Spirit, God's gift, does not want you to be afraid of people, but to be wise and strong, and to love them and enjoy being with them (2 Timothy 1:7, The Living Bible).

Of all our vital relationships, however, friendship is the most fragile. Other primary associations (marriage and kinship) have rights and reinforcements that are missing in friendships. Nothing binds two friends but their desire to be bound. Marriage can summon the law and kinships can rely on the culture to hold relatives together, but friends can walk away any time they want to. It's the commitment to stay together in the midst of this freedom that makes friendship seem sacred. In the company of true friends we tread on holy ground.

10

As I was preparing to write this book, I was also studying one of the New Testament's littlest books: Paul's letter to his friend Philemon. What a timely illustration this epistle offers. It's a letter from one friend to another friend on behalf of a third friend. Paul's concern is to erase the social barriers and accepted prejudices that block full fellowship in Christ. In this letter, I found confirmation of my growing conviction that "spirituality" is not a private experience between a believer and God. Actually, it's a very social phenomenon.

The letter is about a transformed personality. A runaway slave, Onesimus, has deserted his owner Philemon and fled to Rome. While there—we don't know exactly how—he met the imprisoned apostle Paul. Through this providential meeting, Paul introduces Onesimus to the One who will change his life forever. The letter is prompted by Paul's belief that the time has come for the slave to return to his master, but this time, he hopes, on different terms. On behalf of Onesimus, Paul pleads for forgiveness. He urges Philemon to accept Onesimus now as friend and brother.

(By the way, there's an interesting historical footnote I should mention. Apparently, the apostle succeeds. In an early second-century letter of Ignatius, bishop of Antioch in Syria, he refers to the bishop of Ephesus, a man by the name of Onesimus. Most scholars have concluded this Onesimus is the very same man we meet in Paul's letter to Philemon. This is indeed a transformation: from slave to bishop. Being befriended by Paul was the best thing that ever happened to him. He was forever changed for the better. Such is the power of the right kind of friendship.)

Look at just the first three verses of the letter. What they tell us about the meaning of Christian relationships is worth a book in itself. Paul employs five relational terms that introduce the richness of friendship.

The first is **prisoner.**

> I, Paul, a **prisoner** of Christ Jesus, for the sake of you Gentiles. . . .

You have to be as old as I am to remember it, but a popular song of a few decades ago happily lamented, "I'm just a prisoner of love." So Paul. He doesn't consider himself a prisoner of Rome. It merely provides the cell and the guard. Paul thinks of himself as a voluntary prisoner. He's there by reason of his previous decision to become a slave (a prisoner) of Jesus and let the Lord do with him anything He wants. He happens right now to be serving his Master in a Roman prison because that's where Christ wants him. He has long since resigned direction of his life to the Lord. When you give something away, including your life, you are no longer in control of it. Thus Paul is a prisoner of Christ, whom he serves, and not of Rome, *where* he serves.

In every sense, his love has imprisoned him. In Ephesians 3:1, he states it explicitly: "For this reason I, Paul, the prisoner of Christ Jesus for the sake of you Gentiles. . . ." To be a "prisoner" does not at first appeal to an age like ours, which worships personal freedom above all other values. Why would anyone voluntarily give up personal liberty—for anyone? It's hard to take this in, yet if we can't comprehend Paul's motive, we aren't ready for a friendship of our own. Every meaningful bond between persons requires a yielding of at least some freedom.

This fact shouldn't surprise us, should it? Anything to which we commit ourselves restricts us.

> Don't you know that when you offer yourselves to someone to obey him as slaves, you are slaves to the one whom you obey— whether you are slaves to sin, which leads to death, or to obedience, which leads to righteousness? (Romans 6:16).

Total freedom is impossible. All freedom is limited, but we have some freedom to decide how it will be limited. We choose our own prison, actually. Some are confined by passion, others by ambition, still others by addiction. Friends are prisoners of love.

The second word is **brother.**

> I, Paul, a prisoner of Christ Jesus, and Timothy our **brother**. . . .

When a Christian calls himself a "prisoner" of love, he means he belongs to the Lord. The term *brother* announces that he also belongs to certain other people. He has become a member of the family in Christ. And what a family!

Some members of our congregation have taught me how rich this word is by describing a brotherhood beyond the church. Jack Stevens, one of our local firemen, was buried not long ago. Vic and Terry Curtis, two of our members, were very close to Jack, who died when the fire truck he was driving collided with another vehicle just four blocks from our church building. The fire department hired Vic and Jack at the same time ten years before the accident, and the men had become best friends.

After the funeral, Vic and Terry wrote a couple of articles for their professional magazine describing the impact of Jack's life on their own. Three statements from Terry's article say it all. This is the first:

> The funeral made me realize what a truly special entity the fire department is. The ceremony itself was so beautiful and so well organized. Until that day, I never really understood what Victor meant when he would call the fire department a family and his co-workers brothers.

Her next paragraph spoke of Jack Stevens's positive influence and the fact that the death of this vital Christian man sent them in search for the source of his strength. Shortly after the funeral, they were baptized.

Her final paragraph:

> Our son still warns Victor when he begins to talk about the accident and Jack. "You'll make Mom cry," he says. I guess we just need to realize a tragedy like this cannot be foreseen nor completely understood. We just have to appreciate each day we have together and know that our husbands' brothers are always doing their best for each other.

"Our husbands' brothers." Terry uses these words to describe the spirit of mutuality implicit when Paul speaks as a "brother." The spirit in the fire department permeates police departments and military units and every other organization in which people work side by side in mutual respect and dependency. They become like family.

It's the spirit of the church as well. From the beginning, Christians have referred to each other as brothers and sisters.

They become closer than kinfolk. They work together and rely on one another. You often hear a believer testify that his Christian brothers and sisters are dearer than members of his own blood family.

Now for the third word: " . . . to Philemon our dear **friend.** . . ." With this one, we stop for a while. By now, the meanings are beginning to overlap, aren't they? Prisoner of love, brother, friend. Together they point to a special, voluntary, intertwining of personalities.

I can't write about this word objectively. I've become too sentimental. We've just enjoyed a year of reunions, my friends of my youth and I. What a blessed year! Our tour group to the Holy Land included Rosemary Stoltenberg and her husband Carl. Rosemary and I were in the church nursery department together and have remained like brother and sister ever since. George and JoAnn Widmer were there, and Shirley and Harley Christensen, from that same wonderful hometown and church.

My sister and her daughter went along, also, giving these long-separated (by geography) relatives a chance to do a lot of catching up.

Earlier in the summer, my wife Joy and I spent a week white water rafting on the McKenzie River in Oregon with Curtis and Eileen Adams and their daughter Dana. Curt and I were high school buddies, and, when the time came for our weddings, a week apart, we were each other's best man.

There are others, many others, I should mention, friends of twenty and thirty years and more, whose very names bring a smile, who are the reason for this study of friendship. They have deepened and strengthened and enriched my life. One doesn't use the word as Paul does here ("To Philemon our dear friend") lightly. A person with a friend has wealth enough.

To have a friend is to be made better than you would be without one. Good friends elevate your character. As Henry David Thoreau discovered, "A friend is one who incessantly pays us the compliment of expecting from us all the virtues, and who can appreciate them in us. It takes two to speak the truth—one to speak and another to hear." Good friends have power to lift us up—or tear us down. For this reason we never take lightly the friendships we develop in the church. Some folks confess to a virtue they think is a sin. "I'm embarrassed to admit it," they say, "but I sometimes go to church for social reasons." This is cause for congratulations, not apology. Why not look for best friends in the best place? God made us social beings, and He made spirituality a social phenomenon. Doesn't it make good sense that, since you need people anyway, you should hang around the best people there are?

One person admitted, "I've got to get back in church. I need those people to keep me straight." Of course he did. I do. We all do. I counsel newly married couples to be very careful about the friends they choose because their friends can strengthen or weaken their relationships. They—and you and I—need the improving kind.

Catherine Lamb, a special Indianapolis friend, included this bon mot in a recent letter: "I'm reminded of the parable by the Persian poet, Saadi. He was given a bit of ordinary clay, so the story goes. The clay smelled so sweet that its fragrance filled the room.

"What are you, musk or ambergris?" he questioned.

"I am neither," the clay answered, "I'm just a bit of common clay.

"From where, then, do you have this rare perfume?" the poet asked.

The clay replied, "I have companied all summer with the rose."

Some people you company with somehow seem to make you smell better. Others make you stink. Select your friends with care.

Paul's fourth word is **fellow worker.**

". . . To Philemon our . . . **fellow worker."**

As I have already implied, working together is the starting point for many friendships. Our common endeavor draws us together and, in time, usually without our being aware of it, a relationship grows.

A sad incident during the 1948 Olympics demonstrates the degree of commitment of which a "fellow worker" is capable. The French relay team had started well but, as the baton was passed to one of the subsequent runners, somebody dropped it. In an instant, the once hopeful team was out of the race.

15

The guilty runner dropped to the ground, flung his hands to his head, and he wept openly in front of the whole crowd. He kept on crying as he was led from the arena. To some in the stands, it might have seemed unsportsmanlike or unmanly to give way to such emotion. It wasn't. He was a "fellow worker." His error had just wiped out the strenuous effort of the rest of his team. They had counted on him and he had failed them. He had also dashed the hopes of his nation in that contest. No wonder he cried.

Is genuine friendship even possible to someone who can't be that kind of fellow worker? Certainly the church depends on such people. We have our own relay race to run; the baton often must pass from one to another. What happens when it is dropped? We know all too well, don't we?

The last word is the climactic one:

"... to Apphia our sister, to Archippus our **fellow soldier**...."

We're together in friendship, in work, in the family, and as prisoners of Christ Jesus. What makes this togetherness so imperative is that we are at war. Not much needs to be said here, other than to remind ourselves that Christians dare not be only "playing church." We don't assemble every Sunday because it's a nice thing for nice people to come into a nice building and sing nice songs about a nice God. We can't afford this luxury. We are at war.

In Ephesians, Paul speaks of the power of darkness (chapter 6), a power it has never relinquished. The battle for men's loyalties, the struggle for young minds, the fight to feed the hungry and release the imprisoned and rescue the dying and rebuild a world ravaged by war goes on, and Christians are on the front lines. Every time I travel to the third world or behind the Iron Curtain the stark truth stuns me. In many of these places, the Bible is a forbidden book. Some nations decree it a criminal offense to speak the name of Jesus to your neighbor. Many governments turn their guns against their own people, imprisoning them within their own borders. It's wartime on planet earth. The unending battle not only pits communists against capitalists or Arabs against Jews. The real struggle is supranational and supra-ideological. Good is fighting evil in its every form. Lovers of the right, then, have to become fighters together. Otherwise, hatred wins. Along the way, these fellow soldiers become friends.

Here, then, are the five words of introduction to our study. Together they persuade us that the Christian faith is indeed relational. "Spirituality" is not a solitary achievement; it is enhanced and enjoyed through friendship.

---

[1]Leslie Weatherhead, *The Christian Agnostic* (London: Hodder and Stoughton), p. 121.

CHAPTER ONE

Friendship Is for the Wealthy

Philemon; Genesis 13

Hidden in the word *friend* is an often overlooked truth: only rich people can afford to have friends, because friendship is expensive. It costs time, money, energy, and substance. By nature, friendship is extravagant; giving is what it is all about. If you can't or won't be generous with what you have, you will do without friends. If you aren't available to them, they will learn to avoid you. (For this reason, young people generally find it easier to make friends than older people do. They grant greater access to one another; they haven't withdrawn into set patterns of behavior and closed circles of friends, as have many of their elders.)

Paul's addressing Philemon as his "dear friend" subtly prepares Philemon for the costly appeal he is about to make. Paul is going to ask for a great deal—so much, in fact, that only a spiritually wealthy man would entertain Paul's bold idea. He wants Philemon to take back his runaway slave Onesimus without any kind of recrimination. It will cost the slave owner some pride, some loss of face, and the abandoning of some cherished prejudices, but Paul is trusting that Philemon is wealthy enough to do it.

Talking about the high cost of friendship may seem a less than cheerful way to start our study, but we might as well deal with the biggest issue first. (Although I'm no longer a child, to this day if I am forced to eat a vegetable I don't like, I try to gulp it down right away so the flavors that linger after the meal will be the more pleasant ones.) So let's tackle the question of cost immediately.

Here is the fact to be faced: friends are unselfish. They have given up the right to get their way, to hoard their possessions, to control their schedules, to be Number One. Paul is asking

Philemon to forsake all his rights in relation to his slave and, with generosity uncharacteristic of the natural man, to be a friend to Onesimus for the sake of his friend Paul. To give up rights and prerogatives, to offer forgiveness—these are not the acts of an impoverished spirit, but a spiritually rich one.

It's a request one could only make of a person with whom one enjoyed a close relationship. No one else would dare presume. Paul knows Philemon well enough to appreciate the true wealth of the man:

> I always thank my God as I remember you in my prayers, because I hear about your faith in the Lord Jesus and your love for all the saints (Philemon 4, 5).

Any act of genuine, unselfish friendship usually surprises us, making us realize how rare such behavior is—even our own behavior. It's not flattering to me to confess the amazement I still feel every time I reread Genesis 13, the story of Abraham (who is called Abram this early in the Genesis account) and Lot. These two kinsmen had grown wealthy, and "the land could not support them while they stayed together" (Genesis 13:6). The scarcity of food and water was further compounded by the quarreling of the sheiks' herdsmen. Something had to be done.

It was Abraham who took the initiative to resolve the situation; nearly everything he did makes us admire him. Apparently the quarreling didn't disturb Lot, but it did Abraham. It was he who graciously gave the younger man first choice of land to dwell in. Obviously, Abraham cared more about his relationship with Lot than about anything else, including economic advantage.

Lot, on the other hand, pushed his own advantage to the limit:

> Lot looked up and saw that the whole plain of the Jordan was well watered, like the garden of the Lord, like the land of Egypt, toward Zoar.... So Lot chose for himself the whole plain of the Jordan and set out toward the east.... Abram lived in the land of Canaan, while Lot lived among the cities of the plain and pitched his tents near Sodom (Genesis 13:10-12).

There isn't much we can say about Lot that is complimentary. He shrewdly looks out for his best interests without regard to his kinsman. In the brief Genesis accounts (chapters 13 and 19), he comes across as shallow, selfish, grasping, and shortsighted, a man of easy morality.

But Abraham? Everything bespeaks his character. And wealth. He gives Lot every advantage. He seems secure in his walk with God, satisfied he can succeed on his own, and genuinely concerned about Lot's welfare. He is more than kinsman; he is friend.

He is *wealthy* enough to be a friend.

Wealthy in Faith

This chapter is about the wealth that makes friendship possible. Abraham was "very wealthy in livestock and in silver and gold" (Genesis 13:2). Material wealth alone cannot account for his gracious character, however, since Lot, who was singularly lacking in such grace, "also had flocks and herds and tents" (13:5). Everyday experience and documented studies have proved that the materially wealthy are as a rule not nearly as generous as the poor. The wealth that makes friendship possible has little to do with one's financial net worth.

No, Abraham's wealth lay in the richness of his relationship with God (who chose Him both to receive a blessing and to be one) and in his consequent belief in himself. He could afford to let Lot choose first, because Abraham knew he had adequate personal and divine resources to take care of himself.

The contrast between Abraham and Lot gives the lie to the popular "me first" ethic. According to its tenets, Lot should be the hero of the story. He looked out for Number One. He never failed to put himself first. As a consequence, though, his life ended in disaster (read the rest of his pitiful story in chapters 18 and 19). Unable or unwilling to return Abraham's friendship, he acted strictly out of self interest. He reminds us of the words with which the superintendent of the insane asylum in Ibsen's *Peer Gynt* portrays the inmates, who have just been described as being beside themselves:

> Beside themselves? Oh no, you're wrong.
> It's here that men are most themselves—
> Themselves and nothing but themselves—

Sailing with outspread sails of self
Each shuts himself in a cask of self,
The cask stopped with a bung of self
And seasoned in a well of self.
None has a tear for others' woes
Or cares what any other thinks.

Ibsen's words speak directly to our contemporary insistence on self-expression, don't they? In our Hell-bent quest for personal happiness, we demand the right to get what's coming to us and to express what's in us, though in that way lies insanity.

Self-expression. There's a fascinatingly meaningless term for you. What do you suppose we think we mean by it? What is it in our very complex selves we really want to express? Genesis' creation account tells us we are both physical beings, akin to the beasts, and beings into whom God breathed the breath of life. We are earthly and Heavenly, of the dust and of divinity. Which of these selves do we want to express?

Contemporary psychologists refer to our devotion to self as "narcissism." They take the word from the handsome youth of Greek mythology who was cursed by the gods to fall in love with an image he could never possess. Seeing his face reflected in a pool of water, he became so captivated by its beauty he couldn't turn away from it. In time, he became rooted to the spot, and there he remained, gazing forever at the reflection of himself, oblivious to the rest of the world. Sigmund Freud attached Narcissus' name to people whose sole love interest is themselves. They gladly accept—in fact, they insist on receiving—every consideration and favor, but they feel no impulse to return the favors. They are their best, their only, good friends. To serve themselves, they will exploit anybody else. They don't hesitate to trample on the rights of others. They flit from one shallow relationship to another in search of satisfaction that they never can find because they are so much "into" themselves they can never be fully "into" any mutual relationship.

Philip Toynbee, musing on Jesus' command to love our neighbor as we love ourselves, takes mild exception to the assumption that we really love ourselves. No, he says, we cherish and cosset ourselves, scrupulously attend to what we take to be our best interests: nothing is too good for us. To treat another person in this way would do him harm.[1]

It does us harm, too.

So what's the solution? To forget oneself? Probably not, since it is no easy accomplishment to banish from our consciousness the one object of our affection that means more than any other. Rather we should find the true self who deserves expression, not the self of our own devising but the one God had in mind when He created us. That one always remains creature, not Creator; potentially godlike (having been formed in His image), but not god; physically akin to the beasts, but never mere animal; always capable of rising above the grasping, greedy, deceiving, me-firsting person to whom we are so unfortunately attached.

"We should find," I wrote above. Let me change that; the quest "to find myself" is the most futile of all searches. We don't find; we are found. The lost sheep doesn't find himself; the lost son doesn't recover his full self until he loses himself in his father's welcoming embrace (see Luke 15). In a sense, Christ who is the embodiment of our full potential, the visible demonstration of our complete humanity, who is, in other words, our real "self," comes to us, and we who accept Him and are indwelt by Him have then a self worth expressing:

> He was in the world, and though the world was made through him, the world did not recognize him. He came to that which was his own, but his own did not receive him. Yet to all who received him, to those who believed in his name, he gave the right to become children of God—children born not of natural descent, nor of human decision or a husband's will, but born of God (John 1:10-13).

That's the self we want to express, Christ in us. Otherwise, our self-expression may turn out to be merely the exposure of our spiritual poverty.

Wealthy in Morals

This is an awkward phrase, I admit, but I can't think of its improvement. In an era often described as an age of ethical

23

pigmies, rich indeed is the person who knows the difference between right and wrong and acts on it, no matter what. Blessed also is the person who has a friend who likewise knows the difference and can be counted on to act according to his high moral code, no matter what the personal cost.

During his incumbency, President Ronald Reagan enjoyed telling the story of two men who encountered a bear in a forest. As they were running away from him, one man stopped to put on his running shoes. The other one asked him incredulously, "You don't think that, by putting on those shoes, you're going to outrun that bear, do you?"

"I don't have to outrun the bear," he replied. I just have to outrun *you*."

That states the case pretty succinctly, doesn't it? The friend who is not rich in morals, not committed to a standard of behavior higher than his self-interest, cannot really be a friend at all. He'll save his own hide. Period.

As I recall, I first began seriously thinking about this issue of morality in friendship back in those frigid cold-war days when the word came down from high places that we ought to build bomb shelters and store up goods against a Russian invasion. I wondered then what it would be like to have plenty to eat when my neighbor was hungry. Would I feed him? Would I provide only for my family and let him starve? Would I lock my shelter's door against his knocking, letting the enemy get him while I and mine were safe?

I wasn't the only one who thought about such things. Calvin Miller has written of his experience during the Cuban missile crisis. At the time, he was the pastor of a congregation just a few miles from the Strategic Air Command headquarters. As the community wondered what would happen during President Kennedy's embargo of Cuba, in addition to preserving their extra drinking water and food, Miller noted there was a rush to buy handguns and other firearms. Why? Whom could they shoot? The Russians wouldn't be riding their missiles over. There could be only one target for this firepower: neighbors and friends who might have designs on their stockpiled food and water after the holocaust.

The Millers didn't buy a gun. They couldn't picture themselves shooting Harry and Madge, their next-door neighbors. As far as they were concerned, Harry and Madge could have anything they wanted during the crisis. But Miller couldn't help wondering whether, if he needed to borrow "a lead-shielded, isotope-free cup of milk, would Harry have fired on me?"[2]

In a crisis, you learn who your friends are. You learn what their values are. Maybe this is the reason friendship is such a rare phenomenon. Not everybody has the ethical wealth to obey Paul's injunctions to "be devoted to one another in brotherly love," to "honor one another above yourselves" (Romans 12:10), and to "submit to one another out of reverence for Christ" (Ephesians 5:21).

Don't you suspect that even most Christians have a moral code far more self-serving than other-serving? Could we possibly be more like Shirley MacLaine than we will admit? We squirm when we hear her philosophy stated so bluntly—squirm because it accords with our own conduct! In a widely quoted interview in the *Washington Post* in 1977, Miss MacLaine said,

> The most pleasurable journey you take is through yourself . . .
> the only sustaining love is with yourself. . . . When you look
> back on your life and try to figure out where you've been and
> where you're going, when you look at your work, your love
> affairs, your marriages, your children, your pain, your happi-
> ness—when you examine all that closely, what you really find
> out is that the only person you really go to bed with is your-
> self. . . . The only thing you have is working to the consumma-
> tion of your own identity. And that's what I've been trying to do
> all my life.

I do not know Miss MacLaine personally, but from the above I know enough to be afraid of her. If she means what she says, then she's out for herself and herself alone. There is no room in her universe for me. No room for anybody else, for that matter. Her impoverished ethical code has nothing to offer a friend.

Wealthy in Love

In this chapter, *friendship* sounds a lot like *love*. It should. One is the expression of the other.

But not just any love will do.

Students of the Bible have long bewailed the poverty of love-language in English. It can't make the important distinctions among the types of love that, for example, the Greek language is capable of. Our English *love* translates *eros, philia,* and *agape.*

Eros, which gives us *erotic,* is the love of Hollywood and the divorce courts. Rooted in the senses, *eros* is basically self-serving love, the feeling of a person seeking his own good.

Philia is the usual word for friendship or brotherly love (anglophile—lover of things English; Philadelphia, the city of brotherly love). Certainly a higher form of love than the erotic, *philia* is mutual affection, an informal, give-and-take relationship. It is love giving love in the expectation of receiving love. It's capable of sacrifice, but not without reward. An informal, unwritten covenant governs the alliance. Without reciprocity, the association soon dissolves.

Agape is ideal love. It is love that loves whether it is loved or not. The welfare of the other is the supreme concern. It is unconditional, unwavering, John 3:16 love. While we ordinarily think of *philia* as friendship love, which it is, the ideal even in a friendship is *agape.* Even Aristotle, writing centuries before Jesus acted out John 3:16 for us, wrote:

> Friendship seems to consist rather in loving than in being loved. . . . Hence only where there is love in adequate measure, are friends permanent and their friendship lasting.

"Love in adequate measure." That's *agape.* Only *agape* is sufficient to sustain a relationship through all the vicissitudes to which friendships are subject. Such love seeks one thing only: the good of the one loved. The painful truth is that we don't really want to *love;* we want to *be loved.*

This self-serving drive to satisfy our own love needs often makes friendship an elusive goal. When we are always looking for someone to whom we can go and to whom we can tell our troubles, someone who will understand us and protect us against the cruel world, someone on whom we can lean, who will understand and accept us no matter what, we are looking for a friend without first offering to be a friend. There is nothing to build on there. It is really a form of erotic love; it hasn't even risen to the level of *philia,* yet it demands *agape* on the part of the other. It is playing Lot to Abraham, action that blesses Abraham but leads to Lot's destruction. Abraham gains even more wealth, but Lot slips further into spiritual destitution.

Wealthy in Friends

The person, then, who is rich in spirit, rich in morals, and rich in love, will inevitably find himself rich in friends. Friendship is active, not passive. It is giving, not receiving. And even though earlier I used the term "giving up," that phrase is itself misleading because real friendship consists of giving—which is not the same as giving up. In fact, the person who has experienced the truth in Jesus' words, "It is more blessed to give than to receive," has discovered a divine principle. In true giving, you cannot give up. You may give away, but through such giving, you receive more.

That's why I believe friendship is possible only among the wealthy. It begins as an outpouring of a person's spiritual, ethical, and charitable wealth—and ends in the giving person's becoming wealthier than ever. (Can you see why I keep thinking of Abraham? He began wealthy; he became, in every conceivable way, even richer.) It is for this reason that Erich Fromm calls giving "an expression of potency."

> In the very act of giving, I experience my strength, my wealth, my power. This experience of heightened vitality and potency fills me with joy. I experience myself as overflowing, spending, alive, hence as joyous. Giving is more joyous than receiving, not because it is deprivation, but because in the act of giving lies the expression of my aliveness.[4]

Therefore it is not people who *have* a great deal who are rich, but people who *give* a great deal. People who hoard and save deprive themselves of the joy of generosity. They bind themselves to what they have, to what they know, to what they can control. They dwell in a very tiny world. They are poor.

Since they have so little that they are willing to give their friends, they have very few of them. They can't afford many. Constantly looking out for themselves and their possessions, there is no need for anyone else to worry about them. (Who was it who said, "I quit worrying about what people were thinking about me when I discovered they weren't thinking about me at all, but were worrying about what I was thinking about them"?) Since they are looking out for Number One, nobody else needs to. They have chosen to hoard their little wealth, but they are troubling themselves unnecessarily. No one else will touch it. There isn't enough to bother with.

But the truly wealthy have all they need and more. And the more they give, the more they have.

[1]Philip Toynbee, *Part of a Journey* (London: Collins, 1981), p. 329.
[2]Calvin Miller, *Becoming: Yourself in the Making* (Old Tappan, NJ: Revell, 1987), p. 110.
[3]Aristotle, *On Man and the Universe.*
[4]Erich Fromm, "The Theory of Love," *Literary Reflections* (edited by William R. Elkins, Jack L. Kendall, and John R. Willingham; New York: McGraw-Hill, 1982), p. 213.

CHAPTER TWO

Why Friends Cry

Ruth 1:1-18; Mark 2:1-12

Several years ago, Jack Hyles, pastor of the large Hammond, Indiana, First Baptist Church, told this story of a little girl who came up after a baptismal service and asked him to sign her Bible. As he was writing his name, he studied her worn tennis shoes and uncurled hair. He knew she didn't have anybody who cared enough to fix her hair and polish her shoes. There wasn't anybody to ask her when she got home whether she learned anything in Sunday school. Her father was a drunkard and her mother a prostitute, but one day this little girl had heard Jack Hyles tell her he loved her. From that day on, every time she passed him she would tell whoever was with her, "He loves me. He said he did."

The little girl called him "Mr. Brother Hyles." She would say to him, "Mr. Brother Hyles, you are my best friend." She pronounced it "fran." "You are my best fran." His response was a warm hug and a kiss.

One morning she approached him with a long face. "Mr. Brother Hyles, you are my best fran, and I am moving out of town."

He said, "Honey, I am sorry you are moving."

"I said, you are my best fran, and I won't be coming here any more."

"Honey, I am going to miss you."

She became more emphatic. "DID YOU HEAR WHAT I SAID? YOU'RE NOT GOING TO SEE ME ANY MORE, and you're my best fran!"

"Well honey," he comforted her, "I am sorry, and I wish I could see you, and I hate to see you move."

At this, the little girl put her hands on her hips and looked up at him and asked, "Well, ain't you gonna cry?"

And he did. He kissed her goodbye, thinking, "She had no one to love her, no one to care for her."[1]

Caring—that's what friendship is about. Nothing comforts us more than knowing somebody cares. A flippantly tossed "Who cares?" stings as few other words can because, in our insecurity, we often wonder whether anybody does.

A young man seated before the chaplain of a church social agency spoke for a host of hurting people when he answered the chaplain's question, "Rocky, what do you think I can do for you?" Because of a war injury to his back and leg, Rocky had lost his job. He had missed his rent payment, his mother refused to help him any more, and he hadn't seen his wife for many months. At least drinking wasn't a problem, not this time. He was at the end of his rope and had turned to the chaplain because somebody had recommended him. What *did* he expect the chaplain to do?

"I think what I need most is just somebody to be a friend," he told him.[2]

I don't know the young man, but his answer calls from memory the hundreds of people who have said almost the same words to me through the years. They came seeking counsel, but what they hoped to find was a friend. I wish I could tell you that I satisfied their expectations, but I probably didn't. All too often, I sought to isolate their apparent problem, suggest a ready solution, give them a little encouragement, and send them on their way. My motives were good— but my technique was clumsy. I didn't perceive that they hadn't come for help, at least not the kind of help they said they wanted and that I knew how to give. What they were after—friendship—remained an unstated longing, and what I offered—advice—was shallow and, at best, only a temporary salve on an unhealing sore.

I could offer an excuse, of course. Limited time. Limited energy. Pressing duties. Overload.

That takes care of me. But who takes care of them?

There is something else I can do, and I try to do it. Somebody else invented this term, but I have made it my own ever since I heard it: Mine is a "Cupid Ministry." My job is to play the role of matchmaker. Whenever possible, when I cannot remain involved with someone to the extent needed, I arrange opportunities for friendship with someone else to develop.

Everybody needs somebody. In my Cupid Ministry, I try to see that everybody has somebody, somewhere.

Students of church growth have discovered that unless a new member of a church can identify at least seven friends in that church within the first six months, he will drift away from the congregation and back to his former life outside the church. Why? Because in addition to seeking to fill the spiritual void in his life, he is looking for some people who will care about him. He has turned to the church as an antidote to loneliness, or depression—or even despair. If he feels that no one in the congregation cares, why should he remain? He may not know much about theology, but one thing he does know: friends care about each other, and he needs some.

It is the element of caring that dominates in Paul's friendly letter to Philemon. When we read it, we can't help feeling the earnestness of his appeal for the slave: "I appeal to you for my son Onesimus, who became my son while I was in chains. . . . I am sending him—who is my very heart—back to you" (Philemon 10, 12). Paul takes it for granted that his "dear friend" Philemon cares about him: ". . . so that he could take your place in helping me while I am in chains for the gospel" (Philemon 13). Caring—this is what friends are for.

As I am writing these words, my thoughts keep drifting to some of my friends. If I were to describe them to you, I'd begin simply: they care. Some of them, in fact, are friends I would not naturally have chosen on the basis of mutual interests or compatible personalities. Yet they are among my very dearest—because they care so much and let me know it.

What does it mean to care?

Caring Means Taking Risks

When Charles M. Schwab, the famous industrial leader, was 72, he was sued for some trivial matter by a young man he had earlier tried to help. After he finished his testimony before the court, Mr. Schwab asked for permission to make a statement. He said that ninety per cent of his troubles had been the result of "being good to other people," so he advised young people to be hard-boiled and to learn to say no if they wished to avoid the kind of unpleasantness they saw him in. Then he added with a smile, "But you will have to do without friends, and you won't have much fun!"[3]

This one thing you can count on: if you try to be a friend, you'll end up getting yourself hurt. There isn't any defense against it. You can protect yourself from hurt, but only by giving up friends. The truth is that friends sometimes misunderstand you, often misrepresent you, occasionally impose on you, may even misquote you, perhaps outshine you, and certainly will, at times, seem to neglect you. If you can't stand to be disappointed, stay away from friendships. They are risky.

One such relationship I wish the Bible gave us more facts about is the one in Mark 2:1-12. They aren't even called friends, these four men who carried the paralyzed man to Jesus. They must have been, though; who else would have cared enough to go to so much trouble?

The crowded room couldn't accommodate them, but that inconvenience didn't stop them. They carried him to the roof and, piece by piece, disassembled enough of it to make a hole to lower the paralytic through. Imagine the work involved and the social risk they were running for the sake of this man. They persisted in spite of the crowd's probable hostility, the Teacher's possible rebuke, and the utter humiliation they would endure if, in spite of everything they'd done, Jesus couldn't help their friend. As I said, I wish we had more details. One thing is certain: these men cared. So they risked. That's what friends do.

Caring Means Being There

We admire these men. We wish we knew more like them. We are well acquainted with too many of the other kind. I can't forget that eighteen-year-old girl in Indianapolis whose once attractive body was found where she had been dumped in a back alley, face down on the broken glass, the needle marks on both arms and legs a mute testimony of where she'd been.

She wasn't "found," exactly. Police knew where to pick her up. They had been told by a couple of her so-called friends, just before they ran away to leave her to die. When they realized she had taken an overdose, they knew the only way to save her was to get her immediately to a hospital emergency room. To do so, however, meant risking the discovery of their own use of drugs. She wasn't that good a friend, they decided. So they threw her out of their car in the glass-strewn alley and drove off. To salve what little conscience they had left, they anonymously called the hospital to tell the switchboard operator where the girl could be found.

Not exactly a heroic tale, is it?

Friendship takes trouble. It is willing to be disturbed. Safety and ease and privacy are only secondary goods; the primary consideration is what the friend needs. It cares, which means taking risks and being there.

Caring Means Granting Space

Yet we must say a word here on behalf of privacy. While friends are ready to forsake their privacy when the need arises, they are reluctant to do anything that seems to be invading a friend's "space."

There's a hidden qualification in this principle of caring: the care must be wanted. Terrible deeds have been perpetrated in the name of mercy. I learned this firsthand when I was the victim of an automobile-pedestrian accident in downtown Indianapolis. In an instant, I was surrounded by dozens of well-meaning self-appointed authorities, each apparently ready to assume full responsibility for me. They presumed that I had neither the right nor the presence of mind to care for myself. They summoned an ambulance (unnecessary), they forced me to lie on the pavement (unnecessary), and they dispatched me to the hospital (unnecessary) where, among other things, I was forced to spend the night for "observation" (unnecessary). For all of this, I was given the privilege of paying an unnecessarily astronomical amount. Of course, I was grateful for their concern; I only wish they hadn't insulted me by their immediately-assumed air of superiority and their insistence that I could not possibly expect to have any input into the decisions regarding what was best for me.

In that brief encounter with imposed helplessness, I experienced intensely what all of us are all too familiar with—the invasion of our space. Hospital patients and prison inmates suffer this indignity in the extreme. Children of domineering parents—or elderly parents of domineering children—are often likewise victimized. The plight of these unfortunate souls falls outside the scope of this book. I am introducing their problem, however, because friendships are not immune, either. Can a relationship long survive the loss of privacy, the

33

invasion of the all-too-constant companion, the super Samaritan? I doubt it.

We have talked at length about this subject in the Lawson household. Being in the ministry of a fairly large church, ours has been a far more public life than is sometimes comfortable. Each of us has dealt with this loss of privacy according to our individual temperaments, with varying degrees of success. We have compensated at home by granting each other the luxury of some solitude and independence.

This need has influenced our extra-family relationships as well. We form our strongest attachments with people who do not hold us too tightly. They care, but they don't care too much. They are there when needed, constant in their affection but never intrusive. We thank God for them and, oh, how much we need them.

We've discovered we aren't alone. In fact, our need for society balanced by solitude seems to be pretty common. We found a soulmate in author Madeleine l'Engle, who writes of escaping from the pressures of family and career to her secret hideaway out beyond the stone fence and across the high ridge of glacial stone. There, at the end of a trail that leaves her legs marked by the thorns of blackberry brambles and wild roses, is her special star-watching rock.

The "trail" isn't a natural path leading to her hideout. She finds it, in spite of her dim eyesight, by following the twine that she has strung along to guide her way. Her husband laughs about it. "All anybody who wants to find your secret hideout needs to do is climb the stone wall and follow the string,"[4] he says.

That's okay with her. She knows that all secret places are even better when they are shared occasionally. The whole world knows it's no fun having a secret if you can't tell it to somebody sometime. But woe to the person who tries to pry the secret out of you, or who barges uninvited into your sanctuary.

One other qualification must be mentioned here. People who work with alcoholics and other addicts have given us the term *codependendents*. Wives and other persons closely associated with addicts become addicted themselves, not to the drug or alcohol, but to their need to be needed by the addict. They are obsessed with trying to control the other person's behavior, assuming responsibility, devoting themselves so completely to the addict that they lose their sense of identity and self-esteem and, in spite of their best intentions, abet the addiction they hate. They make it possible for the addict to postpone, sometimes indefinitely, the essential facing up to the consequences of his destructive behavior. They carry caring to a disastrous extreme.

Codependency can be healed, but the cure is almost harder to take than the cure for the substance abuser. It is to swear off being responsible for the addict. It requires pulling back from the relationship, forcing the addict to take care of himself. Then the codependent can pay some attention to his (or more typically her) own personality problems. When this happens, the codependent blossoms into a healthier person—one who can more intelligently and helpfully care.

We all need space, the caring healthy who thrive on a diet of society and solitude, and the clinging sick with their codependent caretakers.

Caring Transforms People

The old adage says the longer people are married, the more they look alike. Certainly the more they act alike. They pick up each other's values and schedules and eccentricities. So do very close friends.

The Old Testament story of Ruth and Naomi recounts Ruth's commendable devotion to her mother-in-law. Naomi urges Ruth and her sister-in-law Orpah to return to the homes of their mothers; she is thinking of their welfare. There is no one else to take care of the young widows. Ruth won't leave, though; she doesn't want to desert her mother-in-law. Who would take care of her?

> Don't urge me to leave you or to turn back from you. Where you go I will go, and where you stay I will stay. Your people will be my people and your God my God. Where you die I will die, and there I will be buried. May the Lord deal with me, be it ever so severely, if anything but death separates you and me (Ruth 1:16, 17).

It is one of the Bible's most beloved speeches, often read at weddings to inspire the love of bride and groom. What is seldom emphasized in the services, however, is Ruth's willingness to be changed by her devotion to Naomi. She is giving up her home, her people, her god. She will become one of Naomi's people. Even her faith will become Naomi's. Through her devotion to Naomi's welfare, Ruth will become a different person. The relationship will also change the older woman. Her despair will become joy through Ruth's ministrations, her abandonment replaced by safety and hope.

True friendships do this. Alert parents know this truth; that's the reason they fret over the friends their children choose.

I'm not making a very clever observation, of course. It's a theme the philosophers have long pondered. The Greek slave-philosopher Epictetus's discourse typifies their teachings:

> He who frequently mingles with others, either in conversation or at entertainments, for social purposes in general, must necessarily either become like his companions, or bring them over to his own way. For if a dead coal be applied to a live one, either the first will quench the last, or the last kindle the first. Such being the risk, it is well to be cautious in admitting intimacies of this sort, remembering that one cannot rub shoulders with a soot-stained man without sharing the soot oneself.

The young mother who returned almost desperately to her church didn't know Epictetus, but she had discovered the same truth. "Our friends are dragging us down," she told me. "I understand," I answered, adding that I, too, am more susceptible to influence than I care to admit.

Epictetus's comment about rubbing shoulders reminds me of an often repeated moment of sharing of a much happier kind. It occurs in the baptistry. In fact, my most recent experience took place just a few days before writing this chapter. At the conclusion of our congregation's annual All-Church Retreat, two single adults requested that I baptize them. We borrowed the camp's unheated swimming pool for the breathtaking event. For both John and Maureen, this was really a happy, holy experience; they meant it to be the turning point of their lives. The climax came when, immediately after they were lifted out of the water, they turned and embraced me, an act with transforming consequence for my formerly dry shirt.

Their impulsive act drew me into participation, whether I liked it or not (I did); I was no longer aloof from their experience. I was wet with the same water, happy in their happiness.

Think for a moment of your lifetime friends. How have you influenced one another? To what extent have you had to modify some opinions, alter some conduct, and adjust some habits to meet their expectations? Would you have been the same person without having them in your life? No. Your caring for them and their caring about you has transformed you.

This soot-rubbing characteristic of human relationships has elicited some wise Biblical counsel:

> He who walks with the wise grows wise,
> but a companion of fools suffers harm (Proverbs 13:20).

> As iron sharpens iron,
> so one man sharpens another (Proverbs 27:17).

> And let us consider how we may spur one another on toward love and good deeds. Let us not give up meeting together, as some are in the habit of doing, but let us encourage one another—and all the more as you see the Day approaching (Hebrews 10:24, 25).

Caring Friends Abide

We'll treat this characteristic more thoroughly in a later chapter, but let me introduce the subject of loyalty here because it is such an essential element of caring. It is the crown jewel in Ruth's character: she would abide with Naomi no matter what. It shines in our Lord's character as well: "And surely I am with you always, to the very end of the age" (Matthew 28:20).

Leslie Weatherhead, commenting on people who claim to be avoiding religion because of their intellectual difficulties with it, charges they are frequently hiding behind a lie. He says, "The greatest religious difficulty is not intellectual, but the difficulty of being loyal to the Friend."[5] He insists that the loyalty doesn't break down because of doubts, but because of more "primitive things" like sensuality and selfishness.

What's true in the religious realm is true in all relationships. What breaks down abiding friendships is seldom a flaw in the friend's thinking or a blemish in his personality, but in one's devotion to "sensuality and selfishness."

What, then, enables lifetime friendships to endure when so many others fade away?

Mostly our determination that they shall endure, no matter what.

Mostly our allegiance, pledged and kept through all circumstances.

Mostly the deliberate decision that this time, with this person, selfishness won't intrude. I shall claim him or her as a friend and cling to that friendship against all odds.

Mostly, then, it is my decision that he will be my friend that makes me a friend to him, no matter what he does.

Friends abide. Friends care.

In one of his books, Leo Buscaglia retells the fable of a young girl walking through a meadow when she sees a butterfly impaled upon a thorn. Very carefully she releases it, and the butterfly starts to fly away. Then it comes back and, as these things happen in fairy tales, changes into a beautiful good fairy.

"For your kindness," the good fairy tells the little girl, "I will grant you your fondest wish." After a thoughtful moment the girl replies, "I want to be happy." The fairy leans toward her and whispers the magic formula in her ear. Then she disappears.

The young girl then grows to be a lovely lady, as these things happen in fairy tales, and people all around admire her, for no one is happier than she. When they ask her the secret of her happiness, she only tells them that she once listened to a good fairy.

Even lovely ladies in fairy tales grow old, and when this one does, the neighbors fear she will die and take her secret with her. They beg her to tell what the fairy said. Finally she does.

"She told me that everyone, no matter how secure they seemed, had need of me."[6]

And everyone does.

[1]Retold in *Bus Vision*, a publication of the First Christian Church, Cleveland, Oklahoma, January 24, 1974.

[2]Ralph Bonacker, "The Church and Social Welfare," *Christianity Today*, June 6, 1965, p. 11.

[3]Ralph Sockman, *The Meaning of Suffering* (Nashville: Abingdon, 1961), p. 130.

[4]Madeleine l'Engle, *A Circle of Quiet* (New York: Crossroad [Seabury], 1972), p. 6.

[5]Leslie Weatherhead, *The Transforming Friendship* (London: Epworth Press, 1934), p. 32.

[6]Leo Buscaglia, *Loving Each Other* (Thorofare, NJ: Slack, 1984), p. 14.

CHAPTER THREE

The Tie That Refreshes

1 Corinthians 1:16, 17
Mark 12:28-34 John 15:11

It has undoubtedly happened to you many times. You are reading along casually in your Bible when, suddenly, a certain word stops you cold. You can't go on. The word summons from your subconscious an emotion too strong, too pleasant, or sometimes too painful to allow you to continue reading until you have dealt with it.

That happened to me one day as I came to the close of Paul's first letter to the Corinthians. It's just a casual reference to some friends who have helped him, but "helped" isn't the word Paul chooses:

> I was glad when Stephanas, Fortunatus and Achaicus arrived, because they have supplied what was lacking from you. For they *refreshed* my spirit and yours also. Such men deserve recognition (1 Corinthians 16:17, 18).

They "refreshed" me. J. B. Phillips gives the word even more zest: "they are a *tonic* to me and to you." The Living Bible expands on the nature of the refreshment: "They have cheered me greatly and have been a wonderful encouragement to me, as I am sure they were to you, too."

Such men and women deserve our praise, don't they? What would we do without them? If you are like me, your gallery of friends includes almost every kind. You have some friends you praise for their intellect or accomplishments, others for their physical prowess or beauty, still others for their popularity or unusual talent or special integrity or charm. You are especially grateful to those whose virtues include loyalty, courage, or wisdom. But if like me you are in a "people" vocation with its emotional demands and its constant barrage of criticism, you have learned to cherish those precious, irre-placeable friends who refresh you, whose very presence is a tonic to a tired soul.

Peter uses this word in Acts 3:19. My Bible professor re-quired us to memorize this verse when we were studying the subject of repentance. He did us more of a favor than he in-tended, however, because he introduced us to another kind of refreshment:

> Repent, then, and turn to God, so that your sins may be wiped out, that times of *refreshing* may come from the Lord, and that he may send the Christ, who has been appointed for you—even Jesus (Acts 3:19, 20).

What a delicious insight into the joy of the Christian life this brief verse opens up! We often talk about Jesus as our Lord; we refer to Him as our Savior. He is Master, Teacher, even Friend. But all these titles, accurate though they are, overlook some-thing else that the Lord is to us: He's our Tonic. In His pres-ence we are refreshed, as by a cool swim on a torrid day or a reviving breeze blowing across desert sands. He makes life not only tolerable, but delightful.

They are "*times* of refreshing." There's a touch of realism in Peter's appeal. We can't stay in the water or luxuriate in the cool breeze indefinitely. There is work to be done. We've been called to servanthood. Our service for the Lord will be de-manding; we fool ourselves if we expect to escape drudgery entirely. But we will escape for "times of refreshing." We have a Friend. His presence refreshes us; His service invigorates us.

What Is the Best Thing I Can Give You?

Since I am so dependent upon the "times of refreshing" I receive from the Lord and the tonic that certain friends are to me, I realize that the best thing I can give you, my friend, is a refreshing presence. All you can expect from me is that I will give you what I am, as much as I am. Wasn't it Emerson who remarked that the only true gift is "a portion of thyself"? What else ultimately do I have to give you? Just myself. What kind of self do I bring to you? A bracing one, I hope. I'd like to be a tonic for you, one in whose presence you can relax in "a pause that refreshes." I want you to experience me as a cheerful, giving, very-much-alive person.

I mentioned that my wife and I enjoy the wide diversity among our friends. Some of them, truth to tell, are not exactly refreshing. We have to admit that friendship with them is rather one-sided. In these relationships, Joy and I accept our role as the "refreshers." These friends are rather negative; their dominating characteristic is their uncanny ability to discern—and unfailingly describe—what's wrong. Their characteristic speech is a well-rehearsed recital of woes. They work among imperfect people and they work at unpleasant tasks and they worship in troubled churches and they dwell in the midst of a people of unclean lips and woe is them! When we are together, they feel compelled to update us on all the latest bad news. What do they most need from us? A time of refreshing.

If all our friends were like these, we would perish before long in the spiritual drought. They sap our energy. When they leave, we need a tonic. That is when we praise God that we have some vital, joyful, optimistic, giving friends who flavor our days with gladness. They are to us what Winston Churchill was to Franklin Roosevelt, who sent that famous wartime message, "It is fun to be in the same century with you."

Somebody said that, in Hollywood, if you don't have happiness, you send out for it. I confess I've been known to do the same, but the happiness that's delivered doesn't come in a bottle or a box, but is packaged in the form of a refreshing friend.

One time it came as a convention booklet. Gid and Sally Rudberg from our Arizona church were in Oregon attending the state Christian convention there. Since Joy and I spent the first quarter century of our lives among the Christians in the Northwest, we are always eager to hear any word from home. The Rudbergs, among our most thoughtful—and refreshing— friends, remembered their hardworking pastor and wife slaving away in the heat of an Arizona desert summer while they were luxuriating in the wet, green freshness of the Northwest. They wanted to share the coolness with us.

Sally carried the convention booklet with her and, whenever she saw some of our old friends, she asked them to sign the back page. When we received it, we spent several happy moments reading the names, visualizing the people, and cherishing the memories. There was a note from Joy's parents ("We love you"), a personal one to me from the wife of one of my beloved professors ("Hi! you Rascal!"), another personal one from Dr. Jim Whitaker of our church staff also vacationing in the Northwest ("I signed under duress"). Jess Johnson, who was my minister when I was four years old (and for whom I later worked as youth minister and college vice president), signed the page—and many, many other dear friends. Sally's note was equally treasured:

> "Dear Roy: At the Turner convention we were constantly reminded of you and Joy. So many of your friends were asking about you. Notice their autographs on the back page of my program."

The temperature in the desert that day dropped noticeably. A time of refreshing.

When Paul charged the Ephesians to "speak to one another with psalms, hymns and spiritual songs. Sing and make music in your heart to the Lord ..." (Ephesians 5:19), he wasn't laying down a new form of liturgy for the morning worship service. He was describing those seasons of celebration that come from the Lord and from those who are in the Lord when they get together. Refreshing is the effect of the congregating of dear, uplifting friends.

How Can I Be a Refreshing Kind of Friend?

Earlier today, just before sitting down to write these words, I was reading a national magazine article about Norman Vincent Peale. At more than ninety years old, this remarkable man still walks two miles a day, accepts and keeps speaking engagements all over the world, and as recently as last year went on a safari in Africa (where he slept in a tent like his much younger traveling companions). For years he has been dispensing practical down-to-earth advice for positive living. In one of his books he is right on target:

> Want to be liked? Lift people's spirit. Give them a little extra inspiration. Help build up their strength. They will like you for it. You'll have a warm place in their hearts for always.[1]

To do this, of course, you have to think of them! Even more, you have to decide to like them in spite of any negative traits you perceive in them. You elect to encourage the best in them, even when you are conscious that everything about them isn't the best. You must determine you are going to be upbeat around them, even when theirs is a downbeat. I hope I'm making this clear: you must *decide*. You have to take charge of your own emotions and refuse to allow them to be controlled (or even strongly influenced) by another's negativism. You deliberately act the friend even when the other person isn't particularly friendly. The atmosphere may not change immediately, but in time, as Dr. Peale says, "they will like you for it."

What Matters More, My Happiness or Yours?

This is the crux of the matter, isn't it? A friend thinks of the other person's happiness. In this sense, the basis of the Christian ethic is friendship: "You shall love your neighbor as yourself."

When the lawyer asked Jesus to name the most important of all the commandments (Mark 12:28-34), everyone listening surely expected Him to say,

> Hear, O Israel, the Lord our God, the Lord is one. Love the Lord your God with all your heart and with all your soul and with all your mind and with all your strength.

He was quoting Deuteronomy 6:4-9, the *Shema* (so named from the Hebrew of the first word, "Hear"), the confession of faith that good Jews were expected to recite twice every day.

But Jesus didn't stop with our duty to God:

> The second is this: "Love your neighbor as yourself."

Here He quoted Leviticus 19:18. In the joining of these two Old Testament commandments, Jesus forever made it impossible for His disciples to get away with a purely selfish religion. This requirement distinguishes the Christian ethic from the "me first" ethic of contemporary society. While yuppies boast of their upward mobility and would-be-yuppies may be out to "get theirs," Jesus reduces the grounds of

Christian boasting to two: Do you love God (really), and are you a good friend to your neighbor (and to his neighbor, who is really your neighbor as well, and to his neighbor, who is really . . .)?

Americans feel little guilt about their pursuit of self-centered goals. After all, they reason, isn't the pursuit of happiness one of the stated purposes for America's *Declaration of Independence* from England? Unfortunately (we have to say "unfortunately" when we survey the devastating results of this ethic for egotists), this is true. Thomas Jefferson drew heavily on the writings of philosopher John Locke as he wrote the first draft of the Declaration. Locke had spoken of the basic rights of life, liberty, and the pursuit of property. Jefferson, probably influenced by James Mason, dropped "property" and substituted "happiness." It may sound better, and it certainly appealed to those hard-pressed future Americans who first heard the Declaration, but it doesn't make much sense (and it makes for a terrible social ethic). As a result of this alteration, generations of Americans believe it is their God-given (or at least U.S.-given) right to pursue happiness. Historian Page Smith, commenting on Jefferson's change of "property" to "happiness," calls it an "inspiration." It was undoubtedly unsatisfactory from a "logical" or even a "philosophical" point of view, but it was, he says,

> psychologically right, because it embedded in the opening sentences of the declaration that comparatively new and certainly splendid and luminous idea that a life of weary toil—meager, grim, laborious, anxious, and ultimately tragic—was not the only possible destiny of "the people." . . .[2]

It was psychologically right because it recognized that men and women would fight for personal happiness. They may not know what it is, but they want it. The change of wording was a stroke of political genius. The *Declaration of Independence* was a masterful call to arms.

But by the end of the twentieth century, conditions had altered beyond the pioneers' wildest dreams. What has become of the pursuit of happiness? The fight to overcome the harsh colonial conditions has ripened into an institutionalized individualism that threatens our country with anarchy, and, when applied at the international level, leads our world ever closer to global annihilation. Each citizen demands *his* rights and *his* prerogatives and *his* personal happiness—with little regard for his neighbor or the price his children will pay for his indulgences. He's content to get what's coming to him and leave the overdue bills to the kids. This glorification of the individual, politically approved and legally protected, is anything but friendly to the less fortunate people of our day or to our children and grandchildren.

The English playwright George Bernard Shaw takes issue with the popular interpretation of "the pursuit of happiness" in his play *Man and Superman.*

> This is the true joy in life, the being used for a purpose recognized by yourself as a mighty one; the being a force of nature instead of a feverish selfish little clod of ailments and grievances complaining that the world will not devote itself to making you happy.

Not by any stretch of your vocabulary can you interpret the personal pursuit of happiness as "being used for a [mighty] purpose."

If I seem to have digressed from friendship to the American political scene, bear with me. I am trying to account for the chronic complaining of our countrymen. In this land of plenty, one of the most plenteous commodities is unhappiness. As never before (and as never foreseen by Jefferson and company), Americans are in mad pursuit of happiness. Pursuing, but not catching. In their chase, they are dashing right past their surest shortcut to the refreshment they seek— friendship. They can't reach happiness because they won't be friends. They care more about their own enjoyment than that of their potential friends.

So they run, neither refreshing nor being refreshed.

Is It Happiness We're After, or Joy?

Pop singer Linda Ronstadt has discovered the difference between happiness and joy, according to the newspaper.[3] While recording Mexican music for a new album, she announced that she found it "joyous and triumphant," but, she explained, it isn't "happy" music.

> Happiness is something a woman in Beverly Hills feels when she finds a pink nail varnish to go with her new pink sweater. Mexican music is joyous and triumphant, and joy is an emotion with many components: terror as well as gratitude.

Miss Ronstadt makes a distinction that is often overlooked. Joy and happiness are frequently treated as exact synonyms, which they aren't. She correctly places the locus of happiness in externals, governed by chance; it's in the little things that temporarily brighten one's day. Joy, on the other hand, is deeper, richer, longer-lasting, swelling up from within.

Which is it, then, we are to pursue—happiness or joy?

I mentioned Madeleine l'Engle in the last chapter. This wise woman writes in *A Circle of Quiet* of an evening when she was very, legitimately unhappy. In spite of her mood, she and her husband Hugh had to go to a party. A recently widowed woman was there, quite early in the evening showing signs of too many drinks. She cornered Madeleine, cried into her drink, then suddenly asked her, "You're a very happy person, aren't you?"

Miss l'Engle said at that moment she had every right to be miserable, but she had to confess yes, she was. But on further reflection, she decided the better word was joy,

> because it doesn't have anything to do with pain, physical or spiritual. I have been wholly in joy when I have been in pain—childbirth is the obvious example. Joy is what has made the pain bearable and, in the end, creative rather than destructive.[4]

We must keep this essential distinction between happiness and joy in mind as we meditate on friends that refresh, because joy is the reward of friendship, while single-minded pursuit of happiness is its natural enemy. You can't run off to your personal rainbow's end and give much thought to your neighbor. You can't claim the right to be happy at all costs and at the same time be much interested in whether your friend is or not. Abraham Lincoln used to say, "Folks are generally as happy as they make up their minds to be." People in pursuit of happiness have made up their minds that they don't possess it yet, and they are going to get it come what may. They don't seem to catch on that they are letting their lives be dominated by what's missing.

Joyful persons, on the other hand, are grateful for what they have already attained.

Can I Be Happy if You Aren't?

German contains a terrible word: *Schadenfreude*. It consists of two words, *Schaden* (harm or damage) and *Freude* (joy). *Schadenfreude* is literally enjoying the harm that comes to others. The American cynic Ambrose Bierce doesn't use the German word, but that is really his definition of happiness.

> Happiness: n. An agreeable sensation arising from contemplating the misery of another.

Sadly, Bierce's bitterness is rooted in experience. Shakespeare's Orlando (in *As You Like It*) expresses a common lament: "O, how bitter a thing it is to look into happiness through another man's eyes."

This raises an important question, though. Do you think it's possible to see happiness—better, to be joyful—except through another man's eyes? Can there be solitary joy? Haven't we already established the truth that joy is by definition friendly?

I was thinking about this meaning of joy when word came that a fellow minister and longtime co-worker has had to resign his pulpit because of adultery. When I first heard of it, I told my informant, "I don't believe you." This man couldn't possibly have joined the growing ranks of prominent ministers whose personal lives have been shown to be in shambles. (How often we have been reminded lately that "the spirit is willing but the flesh is weak.") I telephoned, then I wrote. What I learned did not bring me pleasure. Apparently, there was truth in the report.

According to Bierce and Orlando, the news should have made me happy. My colleague was miserable, his career ruined, his sterling personal reputation tarnished, his influence dissipated. This was all a man could want, Bierce would have us believe, to be deliriously happy.

Instead, I was in shock for days, my laughter (what laughter I could muster) forced and my mind so preoccupied that it

49

was difficult to work. I sought a confidant. I had to talk about it.

Why wasn't I rejoicing? Because he was and is my friend. He may be my erring friend, but not my only one. He has lost so much in his fall. I want him to know that at least he hasn't lost this one friend.

Why Does Jesus Place Love Above Happiness?

Jesus nowhere commands His disciples to pursue happiness. He wanted something better for them. He calls it joy.

> As the Father has loved me, so have I loved you. Now remain in my love. If you obey my commands, you will remain in my love, just as I have obeyed my Father's commands and remain in his love. I have told you this so that my *joy* may be in you and that your *joy* may be complete. My command is this: Love each other as I have loved you (John 15:9-12).

Gerald Kennedy tells of a delightful Christian woman with a personality that could brighten the darkest of corners. Someone put that sparkle to the test once by raising a hypothetical question. Suppose, she was asked, when you arrive at the gates of Heaven you are not allowed in. What will you do then?

She said that was an impossible situation, since God had promised to admit all repentant sinners. That answer didn't satisfy, however, so she was again asked for her reaction. "In that case," she said, "I would walk round the walls shouting out that I had had a very wonderful time on the way."[5]

Wouldn't you have enjoyed knowing this woman? She's one of the refreshing ones. How did she have such a wonderful time on the way? There is only one answer. She was a woman who loved life, who loved God, who loved people. She was welcome in any crowd because she wasn't pursuing happiness. She was radiating love. A person like her brings light into any darkness. She was a tonic.

What a refreshing switch from Aristotle's philosophizing. In his *Ethics*, he labors to prove that the final good, the end of life, is happiness. Only happiness, he says, is "that which when isolated makes life desirable and lacking in nothing."

He calls it "the most desirable of all things," the end [goal, purpose] of action."

He's wrong. Jesus knows the heart of man and the mind of God far better, and He defines the end of action to be love: love of God and love of neighbor. For the purposes of this book, we are examining that love (agape) in action. We call it friendship.

Several years ago, William C. Menninger offered "Seven Keys to a Happy Life." Here they are, as adapted by Myron Taylor in his church paper.[6] They offer some practical suggestions for becoming a "refreshing" friend.

1. **Face reality.** Face life as it is and find ways of coping with it.
2. **Adapt to change.**
3. **Control anxieties.** Don't let them control you.
4. **Give of yourself.** We come into the world 100% on the receiving end. Some people have a hard time moving to the "giving" position.
5. **Consider others.** Those who are self-seekers only are most miserable.
6. **Curb hostility.**
7. **Learn to love.**

You've seen many lists like this one. There are only so many variations you can play on this theme. Did you count them? Four of these seven keys have to do with your relations with others. They all place the responsibility for the success of those relationships in your hands. Refreshment comes from loving, not from being loved.

The end of the matter, then, is this: Joy is found in relating to . . . no, we need a stronger word than relating. Joy is found in befriending others. Joyful is the person who has . . . no, that still isn't the right emphasis. Joyful is the person who *is* a friend.

Blessed is the person who refreshes.

---

[1]Norman Vincent Peale. *The Amazing Results of Positive Thinking* (New York: Prentice-Hall, 1959), pp. 73, 74.
[2]Page Smith, *A New Age Now Begins*, Volume I (New York: McGraw-Hill, 1976), p. 698.

[3]*Mesa Tribune*, Tuesday, November 24, 1987.

[4]Madeleine l'Engle, *A Circle of Quiet* (New York: Crossroad [The Seabury Press], 1972), p. 26.

[5]Gerald Kennedy, *Witnesses of the Spirit* (Nashville: The Upper Room [Abingdon], 1961), p. 26.

[6]*The Cathedral Messenger*, published by Westwood Hills Christian Church, Los Angeles, June 26, 1977.

CHAPTER FOUR

Sharing Your Very Best

John 1:40-42; Mark 3:31-35
Romans 1:16

You can't think of friendship apart from sharing; sharing is something friends just naturally do. To a certain extent, of course, sharing is something everybody does, intentionally or otherwise. Without our being conscious of it, we share the air we breathe, the space we occupy, and the nation and culture to which we belong. We share our humanity, our diseases, our fears and anxieties, our hopes, our propensity to sin, and our will to believe. We can't help it.

We can help *how* we share with our friends, though, and we can choose some of the *what*. My good friend Alan Dunbar taught me a good lesson on the subject a few years ago. Alan is the dynamic, frequently mischievous pastor of the Cambrian Heights Church of Christ in Calgary, Alberta, Canada. He invited me to that self-styled Wild West city for a few days of preaching, and I carelessly accepted. Knowing his irrepressible sense of humor, I should have been prepared for the unusual greeting that awaited me, but I guess I just wasn't thinking that day.

As I left the plane and started to make my way to the baggage area, a guard stopped me and pointed out a different exit. I thought it a little strange when he then fell into step beside me, but I didn't say anything. We passed through a door and along a partitioned, temporary, deserted (except for us) walkway. You'd have thought it had been erected just for my welcome—which, it turned out, it had. Across the end was a sign that read:

WELCOME TO CALGARY
ENTRANCE REQUIREMENT:
Minimum Height: 5 ft. 8 in.
(5 ft. 6 in. won't make it.)

When I appealed to the guard for an explanation, he raised himself to full height, cleared his throat, and in his most officious voice read a citation that certified the sign as legitimate and my stature as insufficient. It held out hope for me, though. The restriction could be waived if some trustworthy citizen would be willing to vouch for me. At that moment, the watching Dunbar and all the tall men he could gather broke into laughter.

It was a thoroughly delightful moment. They presented me with a ten-gallon hat that more than made up for my height deficiency, and warmly welcomed me into their guffawing group. I still have a couple of mementos of the occasion, which is why I am reminiscing with you. If you've ever been "officially" greeted in Calgary, you probably have these same souvenirs. The first is a copy of the pledge I was asked to take upon leaving:

> I, havin' pleasured myself considerable, in the only genuine cow town in Canada, namely Calgary, and havin' bin duly exposed to exceptional amounts of heart warmin', tongue loosenin', back slappin', neighbor lovin', Western spirit, solemnly promise to communicate this here Calgary brand hospitality to all folks and critters who cross my trail hereafter.
> Honest Injun! YaHoo!

They also gave me a genuine certificate:

> This here paper proves LeRoy Lawson, being a proud citizen of the only genuine Dad-burned cow town left in Canada . . . name of Calgary . . . has learned how to convey exceptional amounts of heart warmin', back slappin', neighbor lovin', hand shaking and always smiling CALGARY HOSPITALITY. . . . from this day on, owner of this here certificate accepts the responsibility of extendin' said Calgary friendliness among all folks an' critters.

What catches your attention in these examples of Calgarian humility is their unshakable conviction that something as wonderful as experiencing the peerless virtues of their city is not to be hoarded but shared far and wide. If you watched the 1988 Winter Olympics, you heard the commentators exclaim again and again about Calgary's hospitality. They seem to practice what they preach. They honor this fundamental principle of friendship: if you've got the best, you should share it. It's just what friends do.

There's a good example of this magnanimous impulse in John 1:41 and 42. Andrew, who has just made the discovery of his lifetime, can't wait to tell his brother (and friend) Simon his good news. When he hears John the Baptist identify Jesus as "the Lamb of God," Andrew immediately has to share his find:

> The first thing Andrew did was to find his brother Simon and tell him, "We have found the Messiah" (that is, the Christ). Then he brought him to Jesus (John 1:41, 42).

From that moment in the Gospel record, Andrew takes a back seat to his more dominant brother, but if he ever resents Simon Peter's leading role, we never learn of it. He seems content to have played the part of a good friend: he has found the best and shared it.

Andrew and Peter will quickly learn even more about sharing. In an episode that has often puzzled Bible readers, Jesus teaches His disciples about the heightened sense of belonging to one another that characterizes His followers to this day. The Lord seizes an unusual opportunity for the lesson, as recorded in Mark 3:31-35. Surprisingly early in His ministry, Jesus' biological family senses He is in trouble with Judaism's "important people," who have already pronounced Him mad. "He is possessed by Beelzebub! By the prince of demons he is driving out demons" (Mark 3:22).

Mark's typically terse style doesn't explain the arrival of Jesus' family at this moment; it just reports it: "Then Jesus' mother and brothers arrived." That's all. Mark's brief explanation in verse 21 spurs our speculations. Someone undoubtedly has called the family to Jesus' rescue. His wild talk has convinced the authorities He is possessed. He's in serious trouble, His mother and brothers believe, and they think they can protect Him.

Instead of allowing them to lead Him away from the controversy, however, He deliberately intensifies it. "Who are my mother and my brothers?" Scanning the crowd of people now hanging on to His every word, He deliberately pauses. When

He speaks again, His words surprise everyone: "Here are my mother and my brothers! Whoever does God's will is my brother and sister and mother." This is something new. The family circle has always been sacrosanct to the Jews (as to most peoples on earth). Now He brusquely—and none too tactfully—redefines the word's very meaning. His real family is not to be traced through bloodline only, but through spiritual ties. Our relationship to Him and to one another is discovered in acts of obedience, not in genes and chromosomes.

My turning to this episode in Jesus' ministry is itself an indication of the specific kind of sharing that gives Christians our reputation. We share Christ. He's our mutual friend, our teacher, our source of strength. He is, in a word, the very best we have to offer. Like Andrew with his brother, more than anything else we want the people we love to love the One we love. Like Paul, we are not only "not ashamed of the gospel," we too believe "it is the power of God for the salvation of everyone who believes" (Romans 1:16). We want everybody we care about to experience wholeness that comes through acceptance of this gospel.

Leslie Weatherhead has defined Christianity as "the acceptance of the gift of the friendship of Jesus."[1] We are Christians because we have accepted the gift that we earnestly want our friends to accept. Nothing matters more to us. But how can we get them to? Some of them are indifferent, occasionally hostile. They accept our friendship in spite of, not because of, our faith. How can we convince them that we are what we are because of our faith, a faith that could bless them as it has blessed us, if they would let it?

Perhaps another definition would help. The apostle Paul calls the church the bride of Christ (Ephesians 5:22-32). Joseph Aldrich, picking up this metaphor, describes the church as "a *beautiful* bride."

> Ideally, a bride is the epitome of all that is right and beautiful. She's a symbol of purity, hope, purpose, trust, love, beauty, and wholeness in a world pockmarked with ugliness. The bride motif, found in both testaments, is used by God to illustrate His strategy for attracting mankind to the availability of his life-changing grace.[2]

Sometimes our hopes of sharing Christ are dashed because the bride our loved ones have met appeared so ugly to them. It's painful to read, for example, the public journals of the early missionary to the American Indians, David Brainerd. His work was nearly fatally compromised, he complained, by other white men who got to the Indians before he did, not to evangelize but to exploit them. The native Americans resisted him, he wrote in his public journal, "partly from a view of the immorality and vicious behavior of many who are called Christians." "From these white so-called Christians," Brainerd grumbled, "the Indians learned little about the love of God but a great deal about lying, stealing, and drinking."

That wasn't the worst of it; they feared Brainerd wanted to enslave them. What the European white man had already done to the African black man was no secret to the American red man. These "Christians" were not to be trusted. Whenever Brainerd would propose something for their good, they were certain his hidden purpose was to do them ill. The Indian applied this simple, apparently self-evident, syllogism:

a. White men bring evil to Indians.
b. The white men are Christians.
c. Therefore, Christians bring evil to Indians.

They had seen the "bride," and she was not pleasant to behold. They wanted nothing more to do with her. Brainerd's efforts to share Christ with his beloved Indians were utterly frustrated. They had seen too much, and it turned them against the very best he had to offer them. Nothing Brainerd did could erase that image of ugliness.

The moral of the story is pretty obvious, isn't it? The life of Christians in the community of faith must be a thing of beauty. Since most people are lonely and timid, they will be impressed by a church whose members are warm, loving, and generous. They will be even more impressed if those members are eager to extend those virtues to friends (and potential friends) beyond the church's membership. In a generally competitive, abrasive society, no one looks more beautiful than a genuinely caring, sharing person. A church comprised of such persons is attractive enough to gain the right to share Christ with others.

There are many qualities that enhance the church's beauty, all of them deserving comment here, but the limitations of space dictate that I discuss only three of the more appealing traits: openness, purposefulness, and humility.

Openness

A few years ago, I had the privilege of teaching some Christians from Poland, Yugoslavia, and Hungary in Vienna. I'll cherish those weeks for as long as I live. I was supposed to be their teacher, but by their eagerness to learn God's Word, their courage in living daily for Him in the face of persecution, and their joy in singing His praises, I became their student. The Hungarians taught Joy and me one of their sayings (as they lovingly invited us to visit them in their country): "Good neighbors have common gates on their fences." Good neighbors (like good friends) recognize the boundaries between their "personal spaces," but leave an opening for sharing. Robert Frost, in "The Mending Wall," captures our need for both fences and openings when he says on the one hand, "Good fences make good neighbors," and on the other, "Something there is that doesn't love a wall, that wants it down."

We commonly speak of the "*defenses*" we erect to protect our frail egos. "Now don't be defensive," we say when we want someone to be open to a suggestion or criticism. Defensiveness is the sworn enemy of friendship. You can't share and defend at the same time. A friend is one with whom we allow ourselves to be defenseless.

C. S. Lewis said somewhere that "friendship is born the moment one person says to another, 'What! You, too? I thought I was the only one.'" Who hasn't had this experience? But how will another person know what I have experienced unless I am open, willing to share my secrets, daring to be vulnerable? According to Blaise Pascal, the virtue of openness is a rare one. He sounds near despair in these sentences:

> Human life is thus only a perpetual illusion; men deceive and flatter each other. No one speaks of us in our presence as he does in our absence. Human society is founded on mutual deceit; few friendships would endure if each knew what his friend said of

him in his absence, although he then spoke in sincerity and without passion.

Man is, then, only disguise, falsehood, and hypocrisy, both in himself and in regard to others. He does not wish any one to tell him the truth; he avoids telling it to others, and all these dispositions, so removed from justice and reason, have a natural root in his heart. I set it down as a fact that if all men knew what each said of the other, there would not be four friends in the world."[3]

Pascal's is a terrible indictment. If he is to be believed, and I think we may safely doubt him, who would have a friend? There is enough truth to his complaint, though, to cause us to value openness as highly as any other virtue we could name. Combining honesty, integrity, transparency, and vulnerability, openness is a relearned trait. A newborn baby has nothing to hide and hides nothing, but the growing child quickly learns that the art of self-protection relies, as Pascal teaches, on "disguise, falsehood, and hypocrisy." These come to be as natural in the child as biological urges, but the maturing adult must, as Jesus urged, regain something of his former childlikeness. One cannot hope to enjoy friendship without renouncing the machinations of self-preservation and returning to the openness of innocence. This remaking is so radical we call it "being born again."

Purposefulness

Friendships are characterized by mutual tastes and common values, as this book will point out repeatedly, but deeper friendships have an added dimension, a purpose toward which both are striving. This is why soldiers who have once fought death together often remain lifelong comrades. This is also what often binds Christians so closely: they are fighting side by side in a cause they care about with all their being. Their shared purposefulness has brought out their best and drawn them together.

Giving oneself to a purpose can satisfy two parallel, if contradictory, human urges: the need to advance oneself and the need to renounce oneself. Those who jump on a political or religious bandwagon to make names for themselves may very likely achieve their goal, but they will do little personally to convert others to their cause. Those who serve to find release from selfishness in their service, on the other hand, will by their very self-renunciation be effective in winning others, thus advancing themselves as their cause advances. Nothing is more beautiful than self-forgetting devotion to a high-minded purpose.

While I was on a recent visit to England, my friend Bob Wetzel told me of hearing Joseph Tson (pronounced Tone), an exiled Rumanian Baptist minister, speak. Tson said that when his church grew to an attendance of over 1000, the Communist officials interpreted his success as a threat to the government. Secret police hauled him in and beat him within an inch of his life, then dragged him before the minister of cults, who told him his license to preach was being withdrawn. He could either accept assignment to a secular job or be declared unemployed and sent to a work camp.

Tson returned home so deeply discouraged he was questioning his faith. By the time he arrived, he had rationalized that he could still continue to help his church as a layman, but he must give up the pastorate.

When he told his wife what he had decided, her response was unequivocal. "Joseph, I am ashamed of you." She immediately contacted the elderly minister who had led Joseph into the ministry. He came at once.

"Joseph," he said, "you were carrying the standard for us. But now you've put it in the ground and you are hiding in the bushes."

The old man's rebuke revived Joseph's wavering spirit. He became convicted he had to continue. The firmness of his wife and mentor renewed his faith. He went back to the minister of cults and said, "You can kill me, but I am not going to leave the ministry of that church." The official, previously so calloused, seemed a different man.

"Well, let's not talk about killing anyone. Let's see if there is another way we can work this out." Unsurprisingly, he found a loophole in the law whereby Joseph's services could be contracted to the church even though he couldn't be licensed to preach. As it turned out, this provided the way for other ministers whose licenses had been taken away from them, so not only was Joseph able to continue his ministry, but several other ministers were able to resume theirs as well.

When Joseph Tson determined to be true to his purpose, regardless of the consequences, beauty returned to him. When his wife was prepared for any eventuality, so long as her husband would remain faithful, beauty empowered her. When the church responded to Tson's renewed leadership, beauty caused the church's continuing growth. What attractiveness can compare to commitment to a worthwhile purpose?

Humility

It's doubtful a Pharisee, even a Christian one, could lead a sinner to Jesus. When a Christian thinks of himself as spiritually superior, speaking for God, deigning like God to stoop to assist the inferior one below, that poor sinner is going to feel even more miserable. What he needs are not the patronizing ministrations of the pious, but the warm embrace of a fellow sinner. He needs an Andrew.

Peter is such a powerful figure on the pages of the New Testament that, if we aren't careful, we can take too lightly Andrew's importance in the whole story. Without Andrew, Peter might not have become acquainted with Christ. Without Peter, we would be without the first recorded gospel sermon (Acts 2). Without Peter, the gospel would not have been introduced to the Gentiles (Acts 10). In a very real way. Peter had the "keys of the kingdom," just as Jesus promised (Matthew 16:19). All subsequent Christian history, then, acknowledges its debt to the humble, self-effacing man who so eagerly shared his good news with his friend and brother.

Andrew exhibits the "beauty" of humility that is so essential in Christian witnessing. He wants nothing for himself; he merely wants to share the best he has.

Witnessing is easily misunderstood, isn't it? To hear some experts talk, you would think it has to do with memorizing certain laws, repeating certain formulas, or applying certain techniques to persuade your prospective convert to your point of view. Nothing could be further from the truth. Witnessing is much simpler. It has little to do with the act of "being seen" to be a Christian; it is standing beside a fellow sinner and seeing Christ with him. Witnessing is sharing, not showing off. If we are to seek being noticed at all, it is only in a way that fulfills Jesus' wish for us: "Let your light shine before men, that they may see your good deeds and praise your Father in heaven" (Matthew 5:16).

If we are to be observed in our serving, it is only in the spirit captured by the Hungarian poet Endre Adi: "I want to show myself so I can be seen seeing."[4] In my sharing, then, it is not myself I want to share so much as myself in Christ, not my eyes alone but what my eyes have seen, for my friend needs not merely what I have to give of myself but the One whom I have to share, who is himself the best, who will be to my friend what He has been to me. I want my friend to have the best I can give.

---

[1]Leslie Weatherhead, *The Transforming Friendship* (London: The Epworth Press, 1934), p. 25.

[2]Joseph Aldrich, *Life Style Evangelism* (Portland: Multnomah, 1978), p. 25.

[3]Pascal, *Pensees*, II, pp. 100-101.

[4]Quoted in Sylvia Rothchild, *Voices from the Holocaust* (NAL Books, 1981), p. 317.

CHAPTER FIVE

Friends Honor Each Other

John 12:1-8; Matthew 10:8; Mark 2:13-17

We moved recently. I hate just about everything in the process, dismantling, packing, cleaning, loading the truck and unloading the truck, unpacking, getting settled—the whole procedure. My usual sweet, sanguine spirit displays a dark underside that under normal conditions few would ever suspect.

But there is one redeeming feature in this otherwise revolting procedure. Many of our most cherished possessions are gifts from loved ones. Taking them down from the wall or shelf brings back memories of the occasion when a friend honored us with this or that little memento. We pause a moment, give thanks, then return to the work with lifted spirit.

Even this work of writing recalls the faithfulness of my friends Mike and Royce, who dedicated uncountable hours to helping me set up, learn, and work the bugs out of the computer I'm using. I'm a little embarrassed by their generosity— but not so embarrassed that I stop accepting their help.

Friends honor each other in many ways, but especially **by giving to one another.** The monetary value of the gifts has nothing to do with their worth. Among my treasures I have numerous pieces of paper, in various sizes and states of wrinkledness; they are drawings or colorings that some little boy or girl has handed to me after morning worship. Usually they are pictures of me in the pulpit. Sometimes I can't tell that their drawings are exact reproductions of my features, but they assure me they are and I believe them. I thank them, put the gifts in my Bible, and carefully carry them home and praise God for the privilege of being their friend. They do me honor.

If you lack this compulsion to honor your friends by doing things for them or giving them something, your chances of forming a lasting friendship are pretty slim. This was one of Judas's basic flaws, wasn't it? When Mary took the pint of pure nard and poured it out on Jesus' feet and then wiped them with her hair, Judas was horrified. Such an extravagant waste! Such a foolish squandering of a precious commodity! What was the woman thinking? "Why wasn't this perfume sold and the money given to the poor? It was worth a year's wages." John, who tells us this story (John 12:1-8), whispers an aside to let us in on the rest of the story: Judas wasn't interested in feeding the poor but in having the currency ready to hand for his own purposes. Judas was too much the thief to be a good friend.

On another occasion, when Jesus dispatched His disciples on their trial mission, He instructed them to "heal the sick, raise the dead, cleanse those who have leprosy, drive out demons. Freely you have received, freely give" (Matthew 10:8). He added that they weren't to take along any money or other provisions, "for the worker is worth his keep."

His subject on this occasion isn't friendship, but it could be. His purpose is to train His disciples in preaching the message of the kingdom; to do so, He empowers them to befriend those they meet by doing them some good. In turn, He expects that those who benefit from the ministry of His disciples will return the favor by taking care of their needs. His disciples will honor the needy, and the needy will honor the disciples. The beginning of friendship is here.

In a different field, Ralph Waldo Emerson finds the secret of the true scholar in discovering in every man "something wherein I may learn of him; and in that I am his pupil." The scholar gives and the pupil gives.

Giving honor to whom honor is due is so fundamental to friendship that I doubt it can exist without it. Can anyone who is always on the honored, never on the honoring, end for long remain a friend? Friendship requires reciprocity.

Paying honor includes **being positive about one another,** especially in what we say.

> Wouldn't this old world be better
> If folks we meet would say,
> "I know something good about you,"
> And then treat us just that way?

Wouldn't it be fine and dandy,
If each handclasp, warm and true,
Carried with it this assurance,
"I know something good about you"?

Wouldn't life be more happy,
If the good that's in us all
Were the only thing about us
That folks bother to recall?

Wouldn't it be nice to practice
That fine way of thinking too?
You know something good about me,
I know something good about you.
                    (Anonymous)

If the truth were told, every one of us knows something negative about somebody else. We choose, then, whether to concentrate on the negative or the positive. Friends are those who choose to **respond to the best in one another.**

This is what George Santayana calls being "friends in spots." A part of my mind finds union with a part of yours; something in my personality responds to something in yours. You aren't all that I might want you to be—you probably aren't all you want you to be—but I select the best part and pledge my devotion to it.

It has been fun for me to read what some of the world's best thinkers have said on the subject. They are generally in accord, but occasionally I find them at odds. Emerson and Santayana agree, for example, in finding something to learn of another, something to enjoy in another, and befriending that part. The Roman Cicero, on the other hand, dogmatically insists that friendship be defined as "a complete accord on all subjects human and divine, joined with mutual goodwill and affection." By his definition, I have to admit I have very few, if any, friends. I can't think of anyone with whom I am in complete accord on all subjects. All my friends are wrong about something!

But wait a minute. I discovered that Cicero practiced better than he preached. He had a friend named Atticus, described in my copy of the *Harvard Classics* as "generous, amiable, and cultured." So far so good. However, the description continues: "Atticus was not remarkable for the intensity of his devotion either to principles or persons. 'That he was the lifelong friend of Cicero,' says Professor Tyrrell, 'is the best title which Atticus has to remembrance. As a man he was kindly, careful, and shrewd, but nothing more: there was never anything grand or noble in his character. He was the quintessence of prudent mediocrity.'"[1] Whew! Not a friend to boast of, perhaps, yet Cicero found something in him to befriend and pledged his allegiance to that something. It is possible, I suppose, that Cicero kept him around because the "generous, amiable, and cultured" Atticus was also a complete yes man, agreeing with the strong-willed statesman in his every pronouncement. I doubt it, though. While yes men make excellent lackies, they are terrible friends—they will as easily agree with your enemy as with you.

As I said, the truth seems to be that Cicero did better than he said.

I returned from an extended trip to find the card that Judy, my administrative assistant, had left on my desk. There was Charlie Brown's sister Lucy telling me, "It's good to have you back! I was getting tired of being the only perfect person around here." But if I had been perfect, Judy'd be pretty tired of having me around, too! Unfortunately, her flawed boss can't quite make it into the circle of Lowells and Cabots:

> And this is good old Boston,
> The home of the bean and the cod,
> Where the Lowells talk to the Cabots,
> And the Cabots talk only to God.

Although you and I don't belong in that august company, there are enough of us who act as if we think we do, or who pretend to a virtue we don't possess, to have caused the gentle Scots poet Bobby Burns to wish

> O wad some Power the giftie gie us
> To see oursels as ithers see us!
> It wad frae mony a blunder free us,
> An' foolish notion. . . .

But then, as somebody else wagged, "If we could see our-selves as others see us, we'd deny it"!

Like it or not, we're a mixed bag, all of us. If you can't stand to company with sinful and otherwise flawed persons, yours will be a lonely life indeed. You would think the eighteenth century writer Oliver Goldsmith was describing you and me in his *The Good-Natur'd Man:* "We must touch his weak-nesses with a delicate hand. There are some faults so nearly allied with excellence that we can scarce weed out the fault without eradicating the virtue." There's hardly a virtue with-out its vice; but happily, there's hardly a weakness without its strength. Our friends have not aligned themselves with us because they perceive perfection in us, but because, in spite of our limitations (of which they are quite aware), they have decided that our strengths are sufficient to attract them to us in spite of our weaknesses.

The model for such friendship is Jesus. To the first-time reader of the Gospels, Jesus must seem an unusual religious leader. He certainly appeared so to His contemporaries. Many of them rejected Him because, as they observed His circle of intimates and the larger crowd that followed Him, He acted like a decidedly irreligious man. The people of Jesus' nation were looking for a savior. They expected someone sent from God to bring them great teachings and great miracles. Even more importantly, He would rescue them from the tyranny of Rome. They knew what to look for in a savior, too. They never doubted that he would be a religious leader, adhering in every respect to the honored laws of the Jewish people and ac-knowledged by their authorities as he fulfilled their prophets' visions. What they got was a man who did not exhibit the marks of the religious at all. Often He shocked them by casu-ally disregarding some ancient prohibitions, by healing on the Sabbath or attributing to himself some of the prerogatives of God.

In addition, and in some ways even worse, Jesus shocked them by keeping bad company. He stunned religious leaders when He selected as a member of His intimate circle a man nobody else would associate with, Levi (Matthew) the tax collector (Mark 2:13-17). A tax collector (in older Bible trans-lations called a "publican") was a social outcast, a man who bought his job by outbidding others for the right to collect taxes for Rome. These moneygrubbers would charge helpless taxpayers as much as they could get and pocket the difference between what they collected and what Rome demanded. People not unreasonably considered them thieves, extortionists, and traitors to their own kind. No self-respecting Jew had anything to do with such persons. Yet Jesus chose Levi the son of Alphaeus, a man nobody else would have, to be His disciple.

What did Jesus see in him? Loyalty, maybe. Perhaps this man, whom nationalistic Jews considered a traitor, had a capacity for allegiance that his current occupation had covered up. Or perhaps his career had forced him to look for a way back to a God greater than money. Whatever his motive, he immediately left his tax business to follow Jesus, an act of obedience that cost him everything. The fishing disciples could return to their occupation whenever they wanted to. Matthew (Levi) could be a tax collector no more. His trust in Jesus had to be complete. The Lord must have perceived his capacity for loyalty.

Jesus then compounded His critic's confusion by keeping more bad company. He went to dinner at Levi's house. In gratitude for being selected to follow Jesus, Levi threw a party. From Luke we discover that he invited many tax collectors and other social outcasts to the feast. Whom else could he invite? Since eating with a person implied acceptance of and even fellowship with him, only fellow refugees from respectability would attend. He had the temerity to invite Jesus, and Jesus accepted.

Preachers love to ask their congregations from time to time whether they could ever be charged with moral carelessness because of the company they keep. Are they guilty of associating with sinners? It's a fair and important question, isn't it, because the typical Christian mentality is to build our buildings, pronounce our standards, develop our multitudinous programs, and send word out to the world, "If you have any problems or are in need of God, please come in and we will help you. Of course, you'll have to clean up your act first." Jesus' way, on the contrary, was to go and sit where hurting people sat; He went to them. He took all the risks. Rather than condemning them as sinners, He responded to the potential for the good He saw in them.

In so doing, He did as all good friends do. Good friends **bring out the best in one another.**

Philip Yancey tells of a hand surgeon whose insight into this principle led him to do an unusual but inspired act one night. The surgeon was awakened by a 3:00 A.M. telephone call. He was needed immediately in emergency surgery. His specialty was microsurgery, the delicate, meticulous artistry of reconnecting nerves and blood vessels finer than human hairs. The grueling task could take twelve hours without a break. Fighting his grogginess, he impulsively called and awakened a close friend. "I have a very arduous surgery ahead of me, and I need something extra to concentrate on this time," he said. "I'd like to dedicate this surgery to you. If I think about you while I'm performing it, it will help me get through."[2]

Isn't this how it is? If I think about you, or about another very close friend, while I am doing any task, and if I do it in your name, I'll give the job my best. Our friendship will bring out the very best in me. I draw from strength from you.

Jesus said, "And I will do whatever you ask in my name, so that the Son may bring glory to the Father. You may ask me for anything in my name, and I will do it" (John 14:13, 14). That is going friendship one step further, isn't it?

The best that friends bring out in one another is often hidden and even more often ignored. Madison Avenue advertisers study human psychology to discover our hidden lusts and desires. Examine their ads: they appeal to our sex drives, our greed, our pride, our drive for recognition, our fears, and our prejudices, but seldom to our virtues. What advertisers seek to make us less selfish and more giving?

A minister recalls a risky counseling session with a deeply troubled woman. She came to see him in order to get help for her husband, she said. Indeed the marriage did need adjusting, but as she talked, it became clear to him that they could get nowhere so long as her focus was on her husband's shortcomings. Quite abruptly her pastor broke into her monologue and asked her what she was contributing to the dissolution of the marriage. She repeatedly tried to shift the discussion back to her husband, and the minister just as repeatedly returned the question to her. Finally in an outpouring of bitterness, she told him the truth about herself, her feelings, her hurt.

She became extremely angry with her pastor. He realized he could lose her as a friend. He explained that he felt himself to be a very poor counselor but that he wanted more than anything else to be her good friend. That's why he dared to jolt her into seeing what he could see. Following their session, he referred her to a more highly skilled counselor, while he continued to be her friend.

It's a dilemma ministers are often in. When people come for help, does the pastor offer it, even if it can't be on their terms? If he loves them, he must. If they become offended, he will regret their response, but he still must run the risk because, as a true friend, he really does want to help bring out the best in them.

There will be other times, of course, when he can help best by loving them for their positive attributes and saying nothing about the negatives. The secret of wise counseling (and in being a genuine friend) is in knowing when to speak and when to be silent.

Friends honor one another by giving the best they can and by gratefully receiving the best when it is offered.

When I first went to teach at Milligan College in Upper East Tennessee, the longtime former president H.J. Derthick was still living, by then in his nineties. Although he had been retired for many years by the time I joined the faculty, his legend lived on in the many stories we heard about him. One of them was of the time he took his friend J.C. Penney on a trip through the Appalachians. At noon, the travelers stopped at a humble mountain cabin. The owner and his wife rushed to the car to greet their friend and his guest. "Do bring your friend in to have lunch with us, Parson Derthick."

"That is why we are here," Dr. Derthick replied. He had for a long time enjoyed their mountain hospitality.

A chicken was sacrificed and cooked with hot biscuits in the fireplace in the one-room cabin. Dr. Derthick and Mr. Penney sat on the only chairs in the cabin while their hosts sat on boxes. Before they ate, Dr. Derthick was asked to "bless the food."

As they prepared to leave, Mr. Penney offered his host twenty dollars. He refused it. Dr. Derthick said, "Look here, John, this man is a millionaire. He won't miss that bill as much as you and I would miss a nickel."

The proud mountain man straightened his shoulders and answered, "Dr. Derthick, your friend may be a millionaire when it comes to money, but I am a millionaire when it comes to hospitality."[3]

The Lawson family moved from East Tennessee in 1973, but to this day we carry memories of friends like these good mountain folks. Often we were guests in homes of people whose income levels were far lower than ours, but whose hospitality taught us the meaning of "honoring one another." Many visits blossomed into friendships. It is not hard to like someone who is honoring you.

This simple fact may be, then, that elusive secret the friendless seek. Dale Carnegie's courses have always taught that you can make more friends in two months by becoming interested in other people than you can gain in two years of trying to get other people interested in you. This means not envying them, of course, and not competing with them. It requires that most difficult of all disciplines, listening to them. ("The greatest compliment that was ever paid me," Thoreau once said, "was when one asked me what I *thought*, and attended to my answer.")

Perhaps the best picture we can find of this gentle, nonpushy, listening, respectful friendliness is found in, of all unlikely places, the book of Revelation. In contrast to the book's dominant image of Jesus, the Lord presents himself to the church at Laodicea as a meek suppliant, standing outside the door, hoping to be invited in.

> Behold, I stand at the door, and knock: if any man hear my voice, and open the door, I will come in to him, and will sup with him, and he with me (Revelation 3:20, KJV).

Revelation exalts Jesus as the victorious Lord of the universe, with kingdoms and forces and even the devil himself subject to His invincible authority. Yet in this verse, popularly captured in Holman's painting, He honors the sovereignty of the human heart. He wants friendship, but He doesn't force it. As Lord of the universe, He could overrule the individual's self-determination. But He doesn't. He will not force the door of friendship. If His presence is desired, He will go in. If not, He will not.

71

[1]Charles W. Eliot, ed., *The Five Foot Shelf of Books*, Volume 9 (New York: P.F. Collier and Son, 1909), p. 82.

[2]Philip Yancey, *Open Windows* (Nashville: Thomas Nelson, 1985), pp. 111, 112.

[3]The late Mildred Welshimer Phillips, for many years Dean of Women at the college, included this story in *Addresses*, pp. 60, 61.

CHAPTER SIX

The Etiquette of Friendship

Acts 9:32, 36-43
Matthew 25:35-40

You could argue with me about the title of this chapter if you wanted to. You could say it is redundant, since the whole book is about how friends ought to treat one another, and how people ought to treat one another is the definition of etiquette. You could accuse me of belaboring the obvious here, beating a dead horse, or whatever your favorite phrase is.

You could, indeed, and you would be right.

I'm including the chapter anyway. Yes, the whole book is really about friendship etiquette, but I haven't used this term until now. In other chapters, I deal with what we perceive to be larger issues: unselfishness, taking care of one another, refreshing one another, honoring one another, and so on. This chapter is about the little things, William Wordsworth's "nameless, unremembered acts of kindness and of love" that reduce friction in a relationship like oil in an engine. The lubricant doesn't do the work, but without it the engine can't function. A driver seldom pays any attention to his oil level; he would, though, if he allowed it to fall too low.

So would he notice the absence of manners in a friendship. Since each relationship is unique, etiquette expectations are peculiar to each. Whatever they are, though, they are essential.

There is an old Chinese proverb, for example, that needs no elaboration here: "Before fathers and mothers, uncles and aunts, itch as you may, you dare not scratch." My parents didn't quote this Chinese version to us children, but we soon learned that its English equivalent was just as binding. Politeness demanded we observe certain social niceties, and home was the place to practice them.

One of the problems with manners, though, is that they can so easily lead to hypocrisy. Since we can't always behave as we feel, a certain amount of acting governs our behavior. Like Hamlet's uncle Claudius, it is possible to smile and smile and be a villain! Superficial politeness can cover all manner of evil motives. I often find myself going on the defensive, as a matter of fact, whenever any casual acquaintance inquires too probingly about my health or general well being. "Am I being set up? Am I being used? What's he going to ask me for? Has he taken a course in how to make friends and influence people so that he knows he should show some interest in me before trying to get something from me? What's his motive?"

I am not by nature a distrusting person, but unfortunately I've had a little experience. Perhaps that is the reason I am too often guilty of a display of bad manners myself. I don't call it that. I call it frankness or honesty or something else that covers my all-too-often boorish behavior. I overdo my determination not to play the hypocrite. The motive may be admirable, but the consequence is rudeness.

Former Vice President Hubert Humphrey pinpointed our American lack of civility when he noted many years ago that the first sign of a declining civilization is bad manners. Winston Churchill didn't accuse all America of being in such a decline, but he once commented that American Secretary of State John Foster Dulles was "the only case I know of a bull who carries his china shop with him."[1] Judged by English standards of propriety, Dulles failed. Many of my English friends would not single out Mr. Dulles from among the many crude Americans they know. They feel it is a disease that has afflicted the entire nation.

We Americans generally make light of our slipping standards. A common after-dinner joke tells of the woman who, when she boarded the bus, was offered a seat by a man. She fainted. When she recovered, she thanked the man. Then he fainted.

We all agree, I suppose, that, if Hubert Humphrey is right, as a civilization we are indeed in decline. In recent years, political pundits have been speaking more frequently of the "macho" quality in our leaders. When then Vice President George Bush emerged as the Republican candidate for the presidency in 1988, a great deal was made of the "wimp" factor. Was Mr. Bush too gentle, too wishy-washy to be the President? Could he, would he, throw his weight around when the pressure was on? The press threw down the challenge; it was then up to Mr. Bush to prove that he could be just as tough, which often meant just as rude, as the next fellow.

Good grief! How far we've come. How much more wisdom I found in reading the autobiography of Booker T. Washington than in following this trumped up campaign issue through the pages of the daily newspapers. Mr. Washington was speaking specifically of the relations between races, but his words ring true of all leaders.

> My experience has been, that the time to test a true gentleman is to observe him when he is in contact with individuals of a race that is less fortunate than his own.

What is he doing *for*, not *to*, those "beneath" him?

Mr. Washington illustrates his principle with an incident from George Washington's life. The story says that once when General Washington met a colored man [this is B. T. Washington's term, which was preferred in his day as *black* is preferred today] in the road who politely lifted his hat, he lifted his own in return. Some of his white friends who saw the incident criticized him for his action.

George Washington's reply was indeed the measure of the man: "Do you suppose that I am going to permit a poor, ignorant colored man to be more polite than I am?"[2]

Manners, not phony "machoism," dictated our first President's treatment of people.

Our national behavior is not the subject of this essay, however, but our courteous or discourteous treatment of one another as friends. When the Lawson children were small, we tried to teach them that we could even be courteous to one another in the home. We should not take each other for granted but rather extend to members of the family the same kindnesses we would show to guests in the home, or to our friends. The principle wasn't always applied, but we worked at it, anyway.

Dr. Karl Menninger, in one of his books, calls rudeness "a lesser but still important form of violence," a "form of sin." He defines it as "ill mannered and discourteous disregard of amenities and the sensitivities of other people."[3] He relates it to vandalism, which is another of the shapes that intrusion takes.

With Dr. Menninger's definition in mind, we can more readily understand the New Testament's frequent appeals to Christians to be kind to one another (Ephesians 4:32; Colossians 3:12, 13; 1 Peter 3:8). Kindness doesn't come naturally. We have to be "spurred on" to be gentle, helpful, and kind to one another (Hebrews 10:24, 25).

The Bible says very little about the niceties of etiquette. Rather, it concentrates on the attitudes that motivate proper treatment of others. I wonder how many churches have a ladies group they call the Dorcas circle? Peter learned of the gentle namesake of these groups in Joppa. She was famed for "always doing good and helping the poor" (Acts 9:36). She had just died by the time Peter, who was in nearby Lydda, learned of her. Two men came and begged him to follow them to Joppa, to do what he could for their friend.

When Peter arrived, he was taken to her upstairs room. The widows were already there, performing the mourning rituals. They wanted him to see the robes and other clothing that the good woman had made when she was alive.

Peter dismissed everybody, knelt, and prayed. Then he called her by name: "Tabitha [her Aramaic name], get up" (Acts 9:40).

When we study this passage, our attention is usually riveted on the dramatic miracle of Peter's calling her back from the dead. I'm more impressed right now, however, with the picture we are given of this remarkable woman. While alive, she devoted herself to others; in her illness and death, others devoted themselves to her.

She recalls to us Jesus' final words in His great parable of the last judgment (or the sheep and the goats), when the King separates all humanity on the basis of their kindness to others:

> Come, you who are blessed by my Father; take your inheritance, the kingdom prepared for you since the creation of the world. For I was hungry and you gave me something to eat, I was thirsty and you gave me something to drink, I was a stranger and you invited me in, I needed clothes and you clothed me, I was sick and you looked after me, I was in prison and you came to visit me (Matthew 25:34-36).

When these blessed ones protested that they had never seen Him, Jesus answered,

> I tell you the truth, whatever you did for one of the least of these brothers of mine, you did for me (Matthew 25:40).

Jesus' followers have been challenged by this magnificent parable for two thousand years. I myself have preached more sermons on it than I can count and have been instructed and inspired by its words every time. But not until this reading have I applied Jesus' words to my friendships. Whom do I take for granted if not my family and my friends? Who, in terms of my time and energy, are "the least of these" to me? While I am concentrating on the pressing demands of my ministry, am I overlooking my friends? Oh, they understand my schedule. They don't impose. They really don't expect much (which is good, since that is usually what they receive), but have I treated them with respect? Have I been sensitive to their needs? Have I even paid attention when they needed something to eat or drink, or perhaps a word of kindness or a visit when they were imprisoned in their own troubles? Have I?

One of my college students taught me this lesson. She asked for an appointment to see me, but her problems weren't academic. She was discouraged. She explained that she had chosen our Christian college in the first place because she wanted to be in a Christian environment. Then, after she came, she wasn't so sure that it was what she wanted after all. She became restless, felt too restricted. She could hardly wait for summer vacation.

Back home after her first year, she quickly returned to her former ways. She started smoking again and returned to her regular drinking habits. She even allowed herself to be picked up a few times. (I didn't ask what happened then.) By fall, she was eager to return to Milligan College, although when she left after Spring semester, she swore she'd never return.

She came back, she said, because she desperately felt the need for the help of Christian friends and teachers. She was baffled by her need to please people, usually the wrong people. She wanted some Christian companions who would give her the strength to be the person she wanted to be.

This student comes back to mind now because I recall being surprised to learn about this struggle of hers. She appeared to be one of our more popular students, and I never would have guessed just how troubled she was. She was hoping for someone to befriend her, to be kind and helpful, to visit her in the prison of her own spiritual need. She needed help and, until that moment, I hadn't sensed it. I hadn't been much of a friend. I hadn't paid attention to her real needs.

To help us become more attuned and responsive to a friend's needs, then, let's rethink some of the minimum rules of etiquette between friends, ones that aren't being spelled out in other chapters in this book.

1. Be kind and helpful in your own way for your friend's best good. Peter could do the miraculous: he raised Dorcas from her death bed. This is a power the Lord hasn't given you and me. But there are some things we can do—less dramatic, less life-changing, but nonetheless important.

Perhaps I should tell you what some of my friends do for me, just to give you some ideas. My friends realize that I am a mechanical idiot, so a couple of them keep their eyes on my vehicles. Before I know there is anything wrong, they've fixed the problem.

Another friend accuses me of being a financial incompetent. He's right, of course. As a result, I frequently turn to him for advice in money matters. He is as careful with my financial affairs as he is with his own. I know he would never think to gain something for himself at my expense.

There are still others upon whom I rely for assistance in spiritual matters.

You may wonder what I have to offer in return. Not much, I confess. Mostly what I do for a living is talk. To tell the truth, though, there have been a few times when what they have needed is just that: someone to talk for them. I do what I can. And I listen.

2. Keep your mouth shut. As you might guess, this word of advice is for people like me who talk for a living. I recently went with a friend to visit her psychiatrist. While I was quite impressed with the man's expertise, I was equally unimpressed with his enjoyment of his own voice. She had more to say, more that he needed to know before jumping to a quick prescription. But he didn't listen. It's the professional's sickness, this propensity to talk first and listen last.

When Joe Barnett was the minister of the Broadway Church of Christ in Lubbock, Texas, he reported on a conversation he had with one of the officials at Texas Tech. They had just brought in a new football coach, and Barnett was congratulating the administrator on the splendid choice.

"Joe," he answered him, "I hope he can find someone to talk to—someone who won't try to run his football team."

Joe said he knew exactly what the official meant. "Everybody needs someone to talk to—someone he can bare his soul to—*someone who is just interested in him as a person.* There are always people wanting to 'use' the big guy. It's one of the hazards of being a public figure. So he has to be careful who he talks to."[4]

There's the warning to people like me. To be helpful does not mean to be full of advice on how your friend should coach his team or run his business or live his life. More than our good words, people need our better silence.

The conversation reminded Joe Barnett of the well-intentioned but maddening ministrations of Job's friends. They knew exactly what Job's trouble was and exactly what Job should do to get himself out of his miserable situation.

Job pleads with them,

> Have pity on me, my friends, have pity,
> for the hand of God has struck me (Job 19:21).

Job doesn't need their criticism or their endless good advice. What he wants more than anything else is their wordless sympathy. They don't pay any attention to him, though. They think they know what's best for Job. So they keep on talking.

3. Be helpful but not *too* helpful. A friend should respect the desires as well as the needs of his friend.

Charles W. Ferguson, in *A Little Democracy is a Dangerous Thing,*[5] writes of a working man in Leeds, England, whose reaction to certain social reforms, his professional benefactors assured him would be of great value for him, was unforgettable. He said, "But I don't want to be done good to at!"

Christians who really want to be kind and helpful need to remember that sometimes, in fact most of the time, people don't want to be done good to at. "Mother, I'd rather do it myself," is the line from a famous television commercial of a few years ago. Sometimes it's bad to do good, such as

a) when your help increases a person's dependency,
b) when your help embarrasses by exposing weakness,
c) when your help is offered more for your sake than the sake of the other, so that you can feel you've done your duty or gained some "stars in your crown,"
d) when you insist on helping but refuse to accept any kindness offered in return, or
e) when your help increases the other person's sense of inferiority to you.

4. Clean up after yourself. This is such a little thing I hesitate to mention it. I do, though, because anyone whose friend has been a houseguest knows how important a person's respect for the hostess's sensibilities is. You undoubtedly have some friends you love to see come; you also have some others who are a little less welcome. I'm writing this paragraph because of what some harassed hostesses have told me over the years. They tell tales of experiences that would make less noble souls close their homes to visitors for good. Some of their guests have brought along their destructive children (can anyone be more destructive of a friendship than a friend's undisciplined child?); others expect every consideration but grant few of their own. Few budding friendships can survive these seemingly insignificant breaches of etiquette.

5. Remember to say thanks. I remembered to say this because I recently ran across a card that's been in my files for four years. It says it all:

Dear Mr. Lawson,
　　You can't imagine what a blessing you have been to my life through your writing and speaking. Your pursuit of excellence in ministry is an encouragement to me in my own ministry. Sometimes it's not easy for me, and I find myself falling into self-pity and wondering why—but you help put me back into perspective. It's all for the cause of Christ.

I know this is poorly worded, but I hope it at least communicates my appreciation of your work.

Sincerely,

A fellow servant of Christ.

Several things about this kind note I'd like to point out. First, it is anonymous. I receive quite a bit of unsigned mail, almost all of it critical. This is an exception.

Second, the writer is complimentary, and he must be sincere, since he does not identify himself nor ask for anything.

Third, it is simple. He is not writing to impress me but instead is merely thanking me for something I didn't even know I had done for him.

Fourth, the writer knows exactly what I will appreciate. He thanks me for encouraging him and for reminding him that we ministers are serving Christ; that's the true perspective for ministry. I believe this; he knows I believe this, so he flatters me by touching just the right button.

You can see why I've saved it, can't you? It didn't take my correspondent much time to pen this simple thank-you, but here I am, four years later, encouraged to keep on writing because someone, somewhere, was helped. We aren't friends, since he hasn't identified himself to me, but my correspondent knows how to start a friendship if he wants one!

6. Remember to remember. This is one of my biggest breaches of etiquette. I forget. I forget birthdays, anniversaries, and appointments. There is no malice in my poor memory, just thoughtlessness. I'd like to blame my approaching senility, but I've been this bad for years. It's a character, not a chronological, flaw.

There are times when remembering becomes, in the words of an old song, one of the "little things [that] mean a lot." A telephone call to a lonely friend, a personal visit to the hospital or home of a sick friend, a short note to say thanks or to keep in touch. These are intangibles, but they are more to be treasured than any dearly-purchased gift.

When you give a gift, remember the recipient's tastes. I have a friend who has a special gift for gift-giving. He not only remembers all the special days of his loved ones, but he remembers with gifts tailored to them. He has studied them carefully. He knows their likes and dislikes. Instead of getting what pleases him (which is what I am often tempted to do), he ignores his own desires in his yearning to please them.

One more suggestion: give when it is least expected. Holidays and birthdays are obvious times and not to be ignored, of course, but how pleasant it is to receive a surprise gift for no reason at all, except to express love.

The list of suggestions could go on, but I'm running out of space. You don't need more, anyway. Like me, you probably are thinking of many little things you can do, or should not do, that will enhance your relationships. As a friend of mine put it when he explained why he was not going to the latest how-to-be-a-better-minister seminar, "I already know more than I can get done now."

About the etiquette of friendship, most of us know more than we are getting done. We don't really need more advice; we just need to do what we know.

[1]Leonard Mosley, *Dulles* (New York: Dial Press/James Wade, 1978), p. 361.

[2]Booker T. Washington, *The Story of My Life* (Toronto; Naperville, IL; Atlanta, GA: J. L. Nichols & Co., 1901), p. 50.

[3]Karl Menninger, *Whatever Became of Sin?* (New York: Hawthorn Books, 1973), p. 144.

[4]*Broadway Bulletin* (a publication of the Broadway Church of Christ, Lubbock Texas, January 12, 1975), p. 2.

Quoted in *A Reader's Notebook*, compiled by Gerald Kennedy (New York: Harper and Brothers, 1953), p. 276.

CHAPTER SEVEN

Friends Forgive

Psalm 25:1, 7, 11; Philemon 8-22
Matthew 6:14, 15

The older I grow, the more I thank God for grace. Not just His grace, but everybody's. I learned early in my Christian life the impossibility of my ever being good enough or being able to work hard enough to earn my way into God's favor. My salvation had to depend on His goodness, not my own. The Psalmist expresses my own relief:

> Remember not the sins of my youth
>   and my rebellious ways;
> according to your love remember me,
>   for you are good, O Lord (Psalm 25:7).

Of youthful sins I have too many to number. My problem, however, is that although I left my youthful days long ago, I didn't leave my sinning when I said goodbye to adolescence. So even in maturity I can't appeal to my love or my goodness for help.

> For the sake of your name, O Lord,
>   forgive my iniquity, though it is great (Psalm 25:11).

I couldn't ask Him for forgiveness for the sake of my own name, could I? Of what value would my reputation be, since He knows the condition of the character behind the reputation?

> To you, O Lord, I lift up my soul;
>   in you I trust, O my God (Psalm 25:1).

So I begin where the Psalmist begins, and I end there as well. My hope is in the Lord, not in any virtue of my own.

As I said, this lesson I learned early in my Christian life. What I didn't realize for a long time was that the grace that holds me to the Lord in spite of my unworthiness is very much like the grace that holds my friends and me together. We, too, have sinned; we have been less than perfect toward one another. We have disappointed, disturbed, confounded, irritated, and perhaps even been guilty of betraying one another. Yet we are still friends. How can this be possible?

It is possible only because we have forgiven one another. That's grace.

I don't remember exactly when the profundity of this truth first hit me, but I have thanked God for it ever since. I may have been meditating on Paul's incredible assertions in Ephesians 2:5 and 2:8, verses that are the foundation of my hope: "It is by grace you have been saved." By grace. God knows everything there is to know about me. He has seen me at my feeble best and at my humiliating worst. Yet He wants me to be His child anyway. That's grace.

My thoughts on that occasion turned from Him to my wife Joy. Although she may not know me as well as God does, she knows me better than any other human being. When I think of what I have put her through and how I have sometimes treated her, the sins I have committed against her, I blush and repent. As I said, she knows it all. Yet she wants me anyway. That's grace.

And my children? What mistakes can a father make against his children that I have not made? What misunderstandings, what misapplied discipline, what anger they have endured, what disappointments I have caused them to suffer. Yet they want me anyway. That's grace.

My church has been just as gracious. I don't suppose there is an error that a minister can commit that I am innocent of. My judgment has often been faulty, my performance of my duties inadequate, my sermons less than soaring, my counseling inept, and my leadership halting. What charges they could bring against me. But they haven't. They want me anyway. That, too, is grace.

My friends? As I said above, there isn't one of them that I haven't let down in some significant way. When they have needed me, I haven't always been there. They could have demanded more. They could have deserted for worthier friends. But they haven't. They want me anyway. And that's grace.

So I am a Christian by the grace of God, I am a husband by the grace of my wife, I am a father by the grace of my children, I am a pastor by the grace of my congregation, and a friend by the grace of my friends.

The truth is, no long-term relationship can survive without grace, and that requires forgiveness.

This is why Jesus, who cares so much that we love our neighbors as well as God, insists that there is one area in which we have more power than God does. In spite of His great love for us and His desire to do anything to forgive and save us, we can stop Him cold if we want to. If we refuse to forgive people who have sinned against us, by His own statement we make Him helpless to forgive us.

> For if you forgive men when they sin against you, your heavenly Father will also forgive you. But if you do not forgive men their sins, your Father will not forgive your sins (Matthew 6:14, 15).

> And when you stand praying, if you hold anything against anyone, forgive him, so that your Father in heaven may forgive you your sins (Mark 11:25).

To be certain there can be no misunderstanding Him, Jesus tells His story of the unmerciful servant. Surely His disciples, taught from birth the eye-for-eye, tooth-for-tooth ethic of the Old Testament, had difficulty comprehending—let alone obeying—Jesus' demand for radical forgiveness. No wonder Peter, this time speaking for more than himself, asked Jesus, "Lord, how many times shall I forgive my brother when he sins against me? Up to seven times?"

"I tell you," Jesus answered him, "not seven times, but seventy-seven times" (Matthew 18:21-35). The disciples must have gasped. I wish Matthew had recorded their reaction. It couldn't have been much different from what is said in an adult Bible class every time this passage is discussed. We don't want to hear this. We're all for forgiveness, of course, under the right circumstances. Forgiveness is such an admirable virtue—until we have someone to forgive! Then we plead extenuating circumstances.

Jesus drives home His point with His parable. A servant owes his king an astronomical debt, which the king, his heart touched by the servant's pleas and promises, graciously forgives. That very same servant, however, ungraciously tosses his own debtor into prison for failing to repay the pittance he owes him. When the king hears of it, he summons the servant and says, "You wicked servant. I canceled all that debt of yours because you begged me to. Shouldn't you have had mercy on your fellow servant just as I had on you?" This time there is no relenting. The king turns him over to the jailers until he pays back everything he owes (which means he will die there, his debt is so large).

The moral? "This is how my heavenly Father will treat each of you unless you forgive your brother from your heart" (Matthew 18:35). The gospel is God's drama of forgiveness. The cross says it all. The King, to whom we owe more than we can ever repay, has canceled our debts and set us free. There is only one stipulation: that we forgive with the forgiveness with which we have been forgiven. Paul summarizes it in Ephesians 4:32: "Be kind and compassionate to one another, forgiving each other, just as in Christ God forgave you."

It is only because Paul's friend Philemon is a fellow Christian that Paul can even dare propose that he forgive his slave Onesimus and take him back without settling his score against the runaway. According to the mores of the day, Onesimus sinned against his owner. He ran away; he probably filched money from his master to get the means to travel. Paul doesn't plead Onesimus' innocence; he admits his guilt. Then, astonishingly, he urges Philemon to "welcome him as you would welcome me." Forgive him. Extend to him the grace that Christ extended to you and me. I wonder what Philemon's initial reaction was. I know what mine would have been—and I'm a Christian saved by grace, too. How hard it is for us to hold our selfish nature down!

Who Needs to Be Forgiven?

By now the answer is pretty obvious, isn't it? We all do. From little things to big, we trample on one another's feelings more than we want to admit. Our moods, our tempers, our narrow-mindedness, our prejudices, and our preoccupation with ourselves threaten to undo the tightest of relational knots. Bruce Larson tells the delightfully honest story of a brooding friend and his wife. As Larson and his friend were having a morning cup of coffee together, Bruce asked him how he was doing. "Terrible," he told him, and then described the fight he and his wife had had the night before. They went to bed not speaking to one another. He still felt rotten the next morning, but his wife kissed him and said, "Honey, I love you."

It was more than he could handle. He grumped that he didn't love her and he didn't love himself and he didn't love God. In fact, he couldn't think of anybody he did love. But he promised her: "I'm going to pray this morning and I believe that sometime in the near future God will straighten me out because He loves me. He will make me able to love again. And when he does, I promise to put you first on the list!"[1]

With that kind of honesty, there's hope for the relationship.

I have lost count now of the number of books or articles I have read in which the trials of Nazi criminals were described and in which someone recognized with horror that the Nazis were not some half-human half-beastly ogres, but were normal-looking human beings just like us. Charles Colson tells the story of Dinur, whom Adolph Eichman had sent to Auschwitz eighteen years earlier. As Dinur attended Eichman's trial, he began to sob uncontrollably and then fainted during the judicial proceedings. Colson assures his reader that Dinur wasn't overcome by hatred, fear, or horrid memories. "No; it was none of these. Rather, as Dinur explained later, all at once he realized Eichman was not the godlike army officer who had sent so many to their deaths. This Eichman was an ordinary man."

Suddenly Dinur feared for himself, he said. He saw for the first time that he was capable of doing what Eichman had done. He, too, could have sent thousands upon thousands of Jews to their death.[2]

So, just as surely, could you and I. As horrible as it is to contemplate this severe truth, we must. Because we share this sinful nature, Jesus insists that we share forgiveness with our fellow sinners. We need God's grace to forgive us the sins we have committed—and the ones we would commit if our circumstances were different. We can rejoice that grace has delivered us and set us free from sin and guilt; we cannot, however, congratulate ourselves too soon or sing, as some have, of our newfound freedom to do whatever we want:

> Free from the law,
> O blessed condition;
> I can sin all I want,
> and still have remission.[3]

No I can't, and neither can you. At least one sin can block God's forgiveness. We can't withhold forgiveness from the one who sins against us. An honest person won't presume on friendship with man or God. One cannot demand of God what one denies another.

How Do I Do It?

Forgiving is not quite as simple as uttering, "I forgive you." I once received a letter from a lady whom I had unwittingly offended. For many months, she had been avoiding me. Then she decided it was time to let me know exactly how she felt. Her letter was filled with anger and bitterness as she asked me, "Just who do you think you are that you can judge me?" She accused me of playing God, of deliberately doing harm to people around me, and of several other assorted crimes. Then she assured me that she had forgiven me.

But she hadn't. Every sentence of her letter was proof that her rage ran on unabated. Saying the words "I forgive you" is not the same as forgiving. Words come easy; forgiveness is difficult. So how do we do it?

Begin by Accepting God's Forgiveness

As a minister, I frequently deal with people in torment because, though they know the words and have said they believe them, they have really never accepted the fact that they are accepted. God has indeed forgiven them. If their repentance was real and their baptism was not mere ritual, if their faith wasn't feigned, they have full assurance from God's Word that they have been forgiven, no matter how heinous their sin. Their problem is not that God won't forgive them. They won't forgive themselves.

Because they won't, they are unable to extend to others the grace that they have rejected for themselves. They have intellectual knowledge that God has forgiven them, but they think more highly of their own opinion than of God's, and theirs is the sterner standard.

If you are one of them, please read this carefully. Let's agree that you are not a good person. Then let's agree that you are not all bad, either. Of course, you are guilty of some sins you don't want anyone to know about. God already knows them and has made provision to wash them clean through the purifying blood of His Son.

That's right. You are not as loving as you would like to be; you are not as hateful as you could be, either. If you will let Him, God will help you to learn to love as He loves. Open yourself to His loving Spirit and let the Spirit love through you. No matter what case against yourself you put before God, He's heard worse and forgiven worse. He really does love you. He wants to forgive you, to be your friend. If you will let Him, He can put your anxiety about yourself at rest so that you will be able to love genuinely and forgive someone who has done something against you.

Accept yourself. Then you can accept others.

Forgive Them in Your Heart First

Don Cox is the able pastor-counselor at our church. His job is to counsel our members as their friend and pastor. For this task, he is exceptionally qualified, having served more than forty-five years in the ministry. He's my counselor as well; he has taught me a great deal.

He once told me that, in his counseling, he lays down three ground rules with the people who come to see him. If they will agree to these, they can be helped. If they won't, they won't. The rules couldn't be simpler:

1. You must be honest.
2. You must want to change.
3. You must forgive.

Simple they may be, but essential. If you want help, there must be no game playing, no manipulation or deception. Let your aye be aye and your nay be nay. Be honest. If you want help, you must be willing to change. Who wants to? Who isn't comfortable in the old routines? If you want help, you must forgive. Your refusal to forgive is not hurting anyone but yourself. You are poisoning your own system, that's all.

So first, before you attempt reconciliation with your alienated friend, you must decide in your heart that you will do so—and mean it. No "if" clauses—"I'll forgive him if. . . ." No huffing and puffing—"Well, he doesn't deserve this, but I'll condescend and. . . ." No showmanship—"I'll wait until he's in a crowd, then I'll go up to him and. . . ." Nothing but a genuine desire to heal the breach will do.

Forgiveness is not a gift patronizingly extended to an inferior sinner by a superior saint. Like the lady who wrote to me, this nonforgiveness uses the language of reconciliation to widen the breach between the sinless and the sinner. David Augsburger calls this "one-up-forgiveness" and describes it in brittle terms:

> I have examined, weighed, judged you and your behavior and found you sorely lacking in qualities that are worthy of my respect. I have these qualities at this point in time, but you do not. I humbly recognize my superior moral strength and your weakness, my consistent moral behavior and your inconsistency of immorality. I forgive you your trespasses. We will henceforth have a relationship based on the recognition of my benevolence in the hour of your neediness, my generosity in the face of your guilt. You will find some suitable way to be dutifully grateful from this day forward.[4]

Call this what you will, but you simply cannot call it forgiveness!

The beauty of grace is that it not only frees the offender from his load of guilt, it liberates the offended from a crippling spirit of judgment. If it doesn't spring from a generous spirit, it can at least issue from a person with too much self-respect to allow the offending party to control his attitude. In this respect, we applaud the woman in Florida who was raped, shot in the head, brutally mutilated, and abandoned for dead. Incredibly, she survived, although the ordeal left her permanently blinded. When she was interviewed on a television program, the host spoke to her of the bitterness she must feel, the "unhealing scars" she would bear for the rest of her life.

"Oh no!" she told him. "That man took one night of my life. I refuse to give him one additional second!"[5]

90

A wise woman. She has surrendered her "right" to get even; she refuses to dwell on her hurt or to find a way to hurt her attacker for hurting her.

Make the First Move

Remember, according to Jesus in Matthew 18:15-17, it is the offended one who has the responsibility for forgiving.

"But," you may protest, "what if he doesn't want reconciliation? What if I'm rebuffed?" You are correct in fearing you may not be successful. There is no guarantee. Without the effort, however, you can be certain the breach will not be healed and your failure to make an attempt will hurt you. There is a chance, though, that you may succeed.

John White and Ken Blue have thought through the several possible results of your effort to be reconciled:
(1) He could admit he's wrong but that it is his own business, not yours.
(2) He could deny it and convince you you're mistaken. This would lead to reconciliation.
(3) He might lie (and you'd know it).
(4) He might deny the charge, leaving you doubting.
(5) He might refuse to discuss it at all.
(6) He might admit it and ask your help. This would lead to reconciliation.
(7) He might admit and freely repent of it. Reconciliation accomplished.[6]

White and Blue's list spells it out for us: reconciliation is not easily accomplished. As I said earlier, no easy "I forgive you" will do the trick. Sometimes, there are genuine differences to be worked out; other times a change of behavior will be necessary. In the beginning and finally, however, there must be the willingness of the offended to forgive. Everything else is secondary.

Remember That Forgetting Is Part of the Forgiving

"To forgive is to forget" is so trite I'm almost embarrassed to repeat the saying here, yet it must be said. If I say I forgive you but savor the memory of your offense in my heart, I am lying. Forgetting is imperative in our personal relationships. And forgetting is not a one-time thing. Paul Tillich helped me to understand that "forgiving presupposes remembering." It forgets "in spite of." He is not referring to the act of asking for and offering forgiveness, because he feels that sometimes these rituals can be more expressive of "moral arrogance" by one and "enforced humiliation" by the other.

> But I speak of the lasting willingness to accept him who has hurt us. Such forgiveness is the highest form of forgetting, although it is not forgetfulness. . . . Forgetting in spite of remembering is forgiveness.[7]

This deliberate act of forgetfulness is very difficult, as everyone who has ever tried it can testify.

> Of all affliction taught a lover yet,
> 'Tis sure the hardest science to forget![8]

This was one of the difficult lessons for me to learn as a young minister. I was stunned more than once by people who attacked me without warning. Sometimes, even though I was guilty, the attack was out of all proportion to the offense. I quickly learned to apologize for things I did and more often for things I did not do, and to make amends for sins I had knowingly or unknowingly committed. I became adept at asking forgiveness when I was wrong and when I was right. Smooth relationships demand no less of all of us. What made the situation more difficult for me, however, was that in spite of my strongest inclinations, I could not run away from these people who hurt me. I was still their minister. I was under obligation to love them and take care of them no matter what.

I didn't fully realize in those early days that what is expected of a minister by virtue of his job is what the Lord expects of all of us, no matter what our job. We are forbidden to get even; we are not allowed to run away; we are prohibited from looking for an opportunity to embarrass. We are to be reconciled. We are to serve the very ones who hurt us. We are the disciples of the One who, as they were killing Him, prayed, "Father, forgive them. . . ."

Pray for Them
So we try to pray as He prayed. Prayer not only changes things, it changes pray-ers. It can soften the hardest heart.

You have heard that it was said, "Love your neighbor and hate your enemy." But I tell you: Love your enemies and pray for those who persecute you, that you may be sons of your Father in heaven. He causes his sun to rise on the evil and the good, and sends rain on the righteous and the unrighteous. If you love those who love you, what reward will you get? Are not even the tax collectors doing that? And if you greet only your brothers, what are you doing more than others? Do not even pagans do that? Be perfect, therefore, as your heavenly Father is perfect (Matthew 5:43-48).

The mark of sonship is loving one's enemies; the expression of that love is prayer for one's persecutors (as Jesus prayed for His while dying on the cross). The goal of perfection, the context implies, is achieved through applying a higher ethical standard than the pagans and tax collectors. They love their lovers; Christians love their enemies. They hate their enemies; Christians pray for theirs. They remain unreconciled because they are unreconciling; Christians take their cue from Christ, through whom "God was reconciling the world to himself." He has called us to the same "ministry of reconciliation" (2 Corinthians 5:18, 19).

It was from Him we learned the forgiveness that makes friendship possible.

---

[1]Bruce Larson, No Longer Strangers (Waco: Word, 1971), p. 67.

[2]Charles Colson, Who Speaks for God? (Westchester, IL: Crossway, 1985), p. 137.

[3]Quoted in R.C. Sproul, "Is a Life of Faith a Vacation from Works?" Eternity, February 1988, p. 60.

[4]David Augsburger, Caring Enough to Not Forgive (Ventura: Regal Books, 1981).

[5]Leo Buscaglia, Loving Each Other (Thorofare, NJ; Slack, 1984), p. 93.

[6]John White and Ken Blue, Healing the Wounded (Downers Grove: InterVarsity, 1985), pp. 90, 91.

[7]Paul Tillich, The Eternal Now (New York: Charles Scribner's Sons, 1963), p. 32.

[8]Alexander Pope, "Eloisa to Abelard."

CHAPTER EIGHT

True Friends Never Leave You

John 15:12-17

The title of this chapter isn't very imaginative, is it? Of course true friends never leave you! We define a "true friend" as someone who doesn't desert, no matter what. By the time you have lived as long as I have, you have no other definition. Other erstwhile friends have come and gone. Why aren't they your companions now? Because they—or you—quit the friendship. They—or you—weren't "true friends."

What made the difference between the friendships that lasted and those that didn't? Why didn't your true friends also leave? What has held you together, neither time nor distance separating you? The word for the tie that binds us is commitment. True friends are committed to each other. That's what this chapter is about.

As I have been writing about friendship, I have often thought about the most intimate, most enduring of all relationships, marriage. In a good one, all the attributes of friendship flourish. Unfortunately, modern society has damaged marriage by "romanticizing" it so that young people believe they'll find, and fall in love with, that perfect someone who has been prepared in Heaven for them. Aflame with passion, they'll get married, promise undying fidelity, and live happily ever after. First comes the passion, then the promise.

To get a better view of the subject, we need to leave this Western culture and travel eastward, to India for example. Joy and I are blessed in having several good Indian friends. We enjoy being with them and are fascinated by the communication and obvious love between them. In each case, the partners were selected for each other. They had little or nothing to do with the match. They didn't fall in love; they didn't go through a dating and courtship period; they didn't live together to see whether they were compatible with one another. Instead, their parents arranged everything for them, sometimes pairing them with partners they barely knew—if they knew them at all.

Yet each of these is a good marriage. If you were to ask them how they have done it, they would probably say they simply made up their minds that, since they were in this thing together, they had better make the best of it. And they have. First the promise, then the passion.

They have succeeded because they are committed to the marriage and to one another. Their relationships are as difficult, as satisfying, as complicated as any we arrange for ourselves. Their divorce rates are much lower than Western ones, for several reasons: first, their cultures have little tolerance for divorce; second, they do not expect as much out of their relationships as Americans in this "me first" generation do; third, and primarily, they are committed to making their marriages work.

Commitment. In a sense, this is what all satisfying long-term human relationships are about. We were created as social beings, at our best when we are in mutually satisfying relations with others.

Some of us have trouble making friends because we expect to "fall into friendship" the way we have convinced ourselves we must "fall in love." We think it is something mysterious, beyond our control. To the contrary, lasting friendship, like genuine love, is something we almost never fall into. We decide into it, we commit to it, but we don't fall!

One of my oldest friendships is a good example. I was surprised many years ago when the wife of my good friend told me that her husband had few friends. "In fact," she said, "the only reason you and he are such good friends is that you have worked at it." On that point, at least, she was correct. I had worked at it. I highly respected him and enjoyed being with him. It seemed to me that our affection was mutual; even if it wasn't, I enjoyed doing things for him. I guess I suspected I was giving more than he was to the relationship, but I wanted to, because of my regard for, and desire to learn from, him. I was committed. The years have proved that he was, too. The commitment may have been a little lopsided in the beginning, but it became more equal with time.

The truth is, all of us could have more and deeper friendships if we were less devoted to having our own way or finding our own happiness or advancing our own career and more willing to make that commitment to another, which is the basis of all relationships. Actually, commitment is not only the means by which such relationships are made and sustained but is also the end for which those relationships exist. The relationship is the arena or the means by which we express our commitment to each other. The person who is incapable of pledging himself to an unending friendship with another can never know what it is to be fully human, since we were created (like Adam and Eve) *for* one another. "It is not good for man to be alone."

The very word *commitment* connotes an in-spite-of quality, doesn't it? It isn't necessary to be dedicated to something if that something is easily attained or maintained. We only devote ourselves to something that can be quickly or easily lost. We can lose our faith in God if we neglect to keep it in repair; we can lose our happy home if we take it for granted. So we can lose our cherished friends if we don't really value them and decide to hang on to them—no matter what. It is this in-spite-of-ness that we must explore here. True friends never leave you. . . .

In Spite of Changing Circumstances

"For better or for worse. . . ." I once saw the title of a magazine article I didn't want to read. It was, "How to Get Rid of Old Friends One Has 'Outgrown.'" The very thought is instructive, isn't it? It implies that the significant people in our lives exist to serve us at our current stage of growth and, as we continue developing, we will need a new set of "significant others." People are expendable, to be used, used up, and then discarded. They exist for our purposes, not for their own. When you have what you want from them, and they are no longer useful to you, drop them.

This old verse captures the spirit of such selfishness:

Of all my mother's children
I like myself the best.
When I have been provided for
Then they can have the rest.

One of my dear friends is a marital discard because his ambitious wife needed a different kind of husband to help her advance her career. Another friend received a letter of resignation from a woman who had for many years been her closest companion. She said they could not be best friends any more because of my friend's move to a larger house. She felt the increasing affluence made it impossible for her to keep up, so she dropped out of the relationship. If they couldn't be financially equal, they couldn't be friends.

My friend was dropped because of her increasing affluence. It's more common for the one on top of the heap to do the discarding. Many ambitious upwardly mobile adults take as gospel truth the old cliché, "It's not what you know; it's who you know." So they manipulate the people around them to be in the best position to know the movers and shakers. If they have to sacrifice some old friends to make the climb, so be it.

Lasting friendships cannot survive these ambitions. A well-known Christian leader, who for many years had lived humbly on her modest salary, late in life married a prominent millionaire. Soon representatives of every Christian organization that had ever heard of her came to "make friends" with her. They wanted her money. She once told me she hardly knew whom she could trust. They didn't want her friendship, just her wealth. Soon after being married, she realized how much she treasured her longtime intimates; they had loved her when she was poor. She could trust them not to abuse her now that she was rich.

True friends never leave you or betray you, in spite of changing circumstances.

In Spite of Failing Health

I often think, as I am leading a young couple through their marriage vows, how easy it is to say "in sickness and in health" but how hard to live the words. We probably shouldn't celebrate weddings; the appropriate time for celebration is after twenty-five or even fifty years of marriage, after the illnesses, after the financial reversals, after the children are safely out of the nest, after the laughter and tears and agony of the struggle. Then it is appropriate to celebrate their survival. They were committed.

Nothing is more beautiful than the sight of a very old couple taking care of each other. It's become a habit for them. They gently nag and touch and help each other up and aid each other's failing memories. They have stayed together, in spite of. . . .

There's something touching also about those older folks out on the park benches. They are there every day, feeding the birds, eyeing the strangers, checking up on one another's rheumatism or old war wounds and deciding how the President should run the country. They are friends. They have long memories of the wars of their youth and can't remember what they did yesterday, but they are friends.

They are committed to one another, loyal even when it costs them something. We admire such loyalty wherever we see it, between man and wife, between man and man, and even between man and dog. When we call a dog a man's best friend because of his loyalty to his master, we aren't so much paying tribute to the dog's character as to our human longing. In a lifetime that has experienced too much betrayal, what is more to be treasured than a friend's loyalty? I am able to write this book because, in my lifetime, I have been blessed with friends who have remained loyal through my illnesses and embarrassments and successes. Perhaps that is why I don't have the dependency on a dog (or other animal) that some people have. I have tested my friends and found them committed. In spite of. . . .

In Spite of Expanding Love

Love is elastic. What do you do with your old friends when you make new ones? Throw them away? Find some gracious way to end the relationship? Or appreciate the wisdom in adding "friends bright and new" to "friends tried and true"? Pity the person who is relying only on yesterday's companions, especially if that person doesn't die first. It becomes harder to make new friends as we grow older. (At least, that's what I'm told; I'm not there yet, myself). Because it is more difficult, it is all the more essential.

Our family has been going through its greatest transformation since the babies were born. All three children are out of the nest now. One lives near us in Arizona with her family, but the others are in California and New York State. Distance separates us, as does their need for independence. Just the other day, Joy and I were agreeing that it was certainly good for us (although we gave no thought to this at the time) that we took in "adopted" children over the years. They have helped fill the gap left by the departures of our natural-born ones. Christmas may not be as big this year as it has been in the past, because of the moves, but we will have a good time with several of the adoptees here. We certainly do not love our biological children less; love can't be diluted. We are hanging on to them even as we expand the circle of our love.

I mentioned above that older people seem to have a more difficult time making new friends. I wonder if that isn't because as we grow older, we grow too set in our ways, too comfortable with familiar routines, and far too judgmental of people whose ways are not our ways. Not many people, especially many younger people, meet all the requirements we older folks set for admission into our august company.

You won't have any new friends if you require that they be unblemished. There aren't any of those left. The only one I ever heard about died two thousand years ago. So you'd better make up your mind to accept some less-than-perfect ones. Take counsel from the man Warren Wiersbe quotes who discovered that "what I thought were blemishes in others have turned out to be scars."[1] Let them live long enough, and everybody you know will bear scars, some from childhood, some from adolescence, some from maturity's tempestuous years. Some of them still hurt, causing their bearers to be a little difficult to get along with at times. You'll probably find it easier to put up with their eccentricities, though, when you remember the task they have undertaken in trying to be your friend! One of the most penetrating sentences in Thomas a Kempis's classic devotional study, *The Imitation of Christ*, needs to be framed and placed on our bathroom mirrors, to start every day with this thought:

> If thou canst not make thyself such as thou wouldst, how canst thou have another at thy pleasure? Gladly we desire to make other men perfect, but we will not amend our own fault.

As we long since gave up perfecting ourselves, shouldn't we extend the same generosity to those we would befriend? The spirit of judgment that Jesus finds objectionable in His disciples (Matthew 7:1-5) is equally obnoxious among friends. It will literally poison any union. I may think I am not judging him, I may even tell myself that I don't wish to judge him, but my very protesting that I don't is proof that I do. I think him deserving of the judgment I am withholding, even as I congratulate myself on my spiritual superiority in withholding it.

This way lies loneliness. It is only overcome when I remember my own scars and recall that I am not the easiest person to get along with. Then we can be friends, in spite of the scars on both our psyches. In spite of. . . .

In Spite of Criticism

I ask advice from others
I seldom take it though—
I simply let them give it
Because they love it so.

Here's the rub. Just when I have fully accepted my new friend, an old one will wonder what I am doing in his company! Because my old friend has no commitment to this new relationship of mine, he can see all the more clearly those blemishes that I have now forgiven, and he is not bashful about asking, "How can you stand her? What do you see in him?" It may be jealousy speaking, or concern for my welfare, especially my reputation. We are, after all, known by the company we keep.

Remember the condemnation Jesus endured for keeping bad company? Yet He befriended all kinds, in spite of the criticism, and He loyally stuck with them, in spite of their inadequacies. He himself was sometimes exasperated by their slowness to catch on to who He was and what He wanted of them. ("You of so little faith, why are you so afraid?" "O unbelieving and perverse generation, how long shall I stay with you? How long shall I put up with you?") Yet at their final dinner together, Jesus reassured His closest friends of a loyalty that would be true to them even to death:

Greater love has no one than this, that he lay down his life for his friends. You are my friends if you do what I command. I no

longer call you servants, because a servant does not know his
master's business. Instead, I have called you friends, for everything that I learned from my Father I have made known to you"
(John 15:13-15).

He told them everything; He would give them everything,
including His life. He was their friend, in spite of the criticism they brought on Him. And these unremarkable men,
slow to learn and slow to obey, would shortly be charged with
the task of ushering in His church and inaugurating a great
movement that is still growing to this day. His commitment to
them would pay large dividends.

I seem to be belaboring this point, perhaps, but I am doing
so because I don't know of a greater stumbling block to developing new friends than our critical attitude of others or our
fear of being criticized for the company we keep. Our duty to
a friend is to defend and be the advocate of the one we have
befriended. Even at the canonization of a saint, I understand,
the Roman Catholic Church admits a "devil's advocate" to
speak against the candidate. The church has discovered that
the holiest of men cannot be granted honors after their death
until all the devil has against the person be made known and
weighed. Even a saint is not sinless; the Roman Catholic
Church grants sainthood "in spite of." Well, if saints need
the devil's advocate, then we sinners need the Lord's
advocate.

This is the role of the friend, who knows the truth, who sees
the blemishes cum scars, who is willing nonetheless to stand
beside his loved one. In spite of. . . .

In Spite of Distance

This potential obstacle to friendship is very much on my
mind right now because, as I told you, our children are out of
the nest and many of our closest friends live far away. Our
every move to a new ministry has been painful. We treasure
our loved ones and want them close. In the ministry, however,
you can't always choose where you will live and near whom.

As parents, too, you certainly can't dictate your children's
living arrangements after they have grown. We have experienced all the wrenching that Marilee Zdenek captures in
"Splinters in My Pride":

It was hard to let you go:
To watch womanhood reach out and snatch you
Long before the mothering was done.
But if God listened to mothers and gave in,
Would the time for turning loose of daughters ever come?

It was hard when you went away—
For how was I to know
The serendipity of letting go
Would be seeing you come home again
And meeting in a new way
Woman to woman—
Friend to friend.[2]

We have also discovered, with her, the joy of "meeting in a new way." You can't hold on without letting go—of your children, of your family, of your loved ones wherever.

Joy and I have the same feelings about the small band of Christians with whom we began the Tigard Christian Church thirty years ago. We were with them only six years, yet to this day, when we get together, we pick up where we left off a quarter-century ago. We have remained friends, in spite of distance. This experience has been repeated in Tennessee, and later in Indiana. We often thank God for friends so far away and yet so close.

Jesus' friends experienced the same thing with Him. This must be part of the meaning of those remarkable postresurrection appearances. He seems to be letting them know by His sudden comings and goings that He is never very far away from them. In time, they came to realize that, whenever two or more of them gathered together, He really was with them, though absent in the body. This One who died and rose and then ascended and returned in His Spirit would never leave them. His Spirit was in them and around them and ahead of them. Did the apostles view Pentecost as the coming of the third person of the Trinity, the Holy Spirit, or rather as the return of their own recently-departed friend as a Spirit who would be with them always, even to the close of the age?

Didn't He teach them that nothing could separate them from His love? Even death?

Such is the friendship He offers us.

What do we offer in return? A catechism in the Presbyterian Church begins with the question, "What is the chief end of man?" The memorized answer to be given is, "The chief end of man is to love God and enjoy Him forever." Two words carry us beyond the expected "You shall love the Lord. . . ." The first: we are to *enjoy* God. Not only serve Him, obey Him, sacrifice to Him, be committed to Him, remain faithful to Him, but *enjoy* Him, to revel in His presence, be happy in His service, be glad in obedience, be ready with sacrifices, be eager in commitment, take pleasure in faithfulness. The Christian life is a celebration of friendship with God through His Son.

The second word: *forever.* Of course. Friendship is forever. True friends never leave you, and you never leave your true friends.

[1]Quoted in *Eternity,* May 21, 1982.
[2]Marilee Zdenek, *Splinters in My Pride,* Part One (Waco: Word, 1979).

CHAPTER NINE

Jesus' Friends Reach Around the World

Matthew 28:16-20

When you become a friend of Jesus, you step into a world far bigger than you ever dreamed existed. You can't attach yourself to Him and think small; you can't be serious about your friendship with Him and not want anything to do with the rest of His friends. "A friend of Yours is a friend of mine" becomes your motto. Then you discover that His friends reach around the world. Before long, so do yours.

When my longtime friend Ted Yamamori called from his Food for the Hungry office to ask whether our church would like to have an African preacher by the name of John Mpaayi speak for us, I didn't fully realize what a favor Ted was offering. Brother Mpaayi, a Kenyan Maasai leader, was touring the United States as a guest of the agency so that he could say thanks for aid from American Christians during their recent famine. His message was powerful, and his very presence an inspiration to us. The most memorable sermon preached that day, however, came at the conclusion. It was a visible one.

I invited Dr. Yamamori to come forward to pronounce the benediction. Because I was wearing my cordless remote microphone, I asked him to stand close to me so his words would be carried over the loud speaking system. John Mpaayi was at my other side. As Ted began to pray, I unconsciously put my arms around the back of each of these Christian brothers. Then, in the midst of the prayer, the impact of this simple but highly symbolic act hit me: here was America embracing Asia on the one side and Africa on the other. Instantly I thought of a song I learned in Sunday school:

> Jesus loves the little children,
> All the children of the world.

Red and yellow, black and white,
They are precious in His sight,
Jesus loves the little children of the world.

Not only does Jesus love them, but He loves them through His church. That day we saw how His love works. The Japanese president of an international Christian benevolent agency prayed for an African whose people had received the assistance offered by American Christians. There were black and yellow and white in a holy embrace.

I said when you become a Christian, you step into a much larger world. That's the truth. So, on the other hand, is its contradiction: when you become a Christian, the world becomes much smaller for you. Thanks to your love for Jesus' friends around the world, Africa doesn't seem so foreign to you anymore, and Asia comes much closer through the Christians you know there. When on television's evening news you see violence in the Union of South Africa or rioting in a Central American state, you can't be indifferent because you know that Jesus' friends live there, too, and what happens to them matters to Him—and to you!

Since that memorable day at Central Christian Church, I have not been able to see John Mpaayi again, although his ministry is well known to many American church leaders. I have met other Maasai Christians, though. While in Maasailand, I saw a similar symbol of Christian brotherhood. It happened that Phil Blowers of Indianapolis and I were in Kenya as guests of Dr. Yamamori. On a Sunday morning, while the more than 2,000 Central Christian worshipers were gathered in our beautiful air-conditioned building in the Arizona desert, I was standing in another desert, under a thorn tree, preaching to a congregation of about sixty. Sitting among those handsome, earnest black believers were missionaries Phil and Gwen Hudson and their young son and daughter. Only the Hudson children's white skin distinguished them from the other youngsters. "Red and yellow, black and white, they are precious. . . ." Then another unforgettable benediction. Once more Africa and America and Asia were joined, this time under a Kenyan thorn tree. We were all Jesus' friends, learning how to be each others' friends.

Only two weeks following this incident, I was in another country. Three days after Ted, Phil, and I returned from Africa, Joy and I left with a group of pilgrims for the Holy Land. En route, we stopped in Athens for our plane to be serviced. We were asked (no, it was stronger than that—we were ordered) to remain on board. The words were unnecessary, since our plane stopped at the far edge of the tarmac, a safe distance from the terminal. We looked out our window to see a mini-tank with a couple of soldiers manning machine guns aimed directly at us. Having visited several third-world and communist countries, the sight didn't strike Joy and me as unusual, but many of our party squirmed uncomfortably. It was their first taste of the armed suspicion with which nervous governments view aliens.

Guns have been aimed at the Lawsons at the borders of several hostile countries through the years. At first, they alarmed us. Not anymore. By now we have learned that once we pass beyond the government's inhospitable checkpoints, we'll find Christians on the other side. They don't know us yet, but they will befriend us anyway, because we have a mutual Friend. In this world, we are citizens of nations that distrust one another; fortunately, we hold dual citizenships. We belong to a kingdom above nations, where neither passport nor borders nor checkpoints exist; where love and peace and friendship prevail. Behind the borders of every country we have visited on earth, we have found citizens of this Heavenly kingdom. With them we are at home among friends.

The philosopher Santayana once commented on Charles Dickens's impact on his reading audience. He listed the author's many defects, such as his indifference regarding religion, science, politics, and art, but concluded nonetheless that Charles Dickens is "one of the best friends mankind has ever had." As a longtime fan of the Victorian novelist (as a grown man, I still cry through some of those tender moments in *Great Expectations* and *David Copperfield*), I agree with Santayana's praise of Dickens. But when the author's influence is compared with that of Jesus, his assessment is revealed for the exaggeration it is. Friends of Dickens are a small and steadily diminishing number. They share a love for the man, but they give little evidence of loving those the man loved.

Friends of Jesus, however, are an ever-increasing band of comrades whose association stimulates not only their intellect but their emotions, their wills, their everything. Jesus is not a comfortable buddy whose teachings invite you and another fan to curl up in your easy chairs before the fireplace and chat with one another about your favorite passages. To the contrary: He makes you uncomfortable with your comfort. He persistently reminds you He has other friends out there in the cold. He urges you to forsake your easy chair and go to them, whatever their circumstances. Jesus' friends don't relax around the club fireplace; they gather briefly beneath a cross, then step out into a bigger world.

Jesus' formal instructions are well known:

> Go and make disciples of all nations, baptizing them in the name of the Father and of the Son and of the Holy Spirit, and teaching them to obey everything I have commanded you. And surely I am with you always, to the very end of the age (Matthew 28:19, 20).

You can't mistake His intent, can you?

We tend to interpret this Great Commission as a call to leave our own nation and serve in another. It may be that for us, or it may point us to more dedicated service at home, wherever home is.

While in Africa, our group met Humphrey Siskuku, a humble minister to people subsisting on a former 20,000-acre colonial ranch outside Nairobi. Converted to Christ as a young man, Humphrey attended Bible college to prepare for the ministry. While there, he learned of Ruai and the extreme poverty killing at least two children a month there. Those who escaped starvation couldn't avoid illiteracy, since they weren't allowed to attend school without a uniform, but their parents were too poor to provide them. The circle was unbroken: poverty ... hunger ... illiteracy ... more poverty ... more hunger.... These people needed a friend. Humphrey and a group of other Christians asked God for a pastor for Ruai. When he opened his eyes, he discovered the hands of his fellow petitioners resting on him. God was calling him to befriend the people of Ruai. He obeyed the call. Thanks to Brother Siskuku, the people we visited had hope. We watched women making uniforms poor parents could afford to buy for their children. The pastor has cooperated with Food for the Hungry to introduce the manufacturing of a fence-making device so the men could earn some money. As their minister, Humphrey teaches them about Jesus at the same time he organizes the community to improve their standard of living. He is carrying out Jesus' commission in his homeland, as his people's friend. In Jesus' name.

We won't forget Terry Allenbaugh, either. A Missionary Aviation Fellowship pilot, Terry and his family were living in Addis Ababa at the time, although Terry wasn't home a great deal. He was working long days, flying grain to the remotest regions of northern Ethiopia, doing his part to stave off the starvation threatening millions of lives. We flew with Terry in an unforgettable crocodile-sighting expedition along the Blue Nile River. He impressed us with his aviational skill, but more importantly, we felt his compassion for the hurting people whose lives he was helping to save, most of whom wouldn't ever know who he was. He was just the faceless pilot in the grain-bearing plane. Terry is a Christian who believes Jesus loves them, so he has befriended them in His name.

In Africa, we met many Christians who had done time in prison for their faith. Some have extraordinary tales to tell. One man speaks of his four-year prison term as his "vacation," and thanks God for the blessings he received there. One of the greatest was the opportunity of leading a high government official to Christ. The official, incarcerated for some infraction or other, was well supplied with food and drink by his family. While he indulged himself liberally of both, he couldn't help noticing that the Christian wasn't drinking. When he asked him why, the Christian explained he refrained because of his religious convictions. His fellow prisoner's question gave him an opening, and he testified to the official concerning what being a friend of Christ meant to him. In time, he led the official to the Lord.

The church is officially banned in many countries, banned but not banished. In most of these countries, an underground church flourishes. The reason is not hard to discover. While the government exploits its people, the friends of Jesus are quietly, courageously doing everything they can to serve them.

As you have probably detected by now, I am writing this chapter while once again visiting Christians abroad. My church has a generous sabbatical program for the ministers, and this year it's my turn to take a four-month leave. Because of the church's strong commitment to missions, my sabbatical has been dedicated to a ministry of encouragement to our brothers and sisters in other countries. Joy has been able to accompany me on some of the trips. From the Bolivian Andes and Peruvian jungles to rural India and urban England, we have been meeting and praying with fellow Christians, most of whom we have not met before these trips but whom we shall now never forget. We have become friends, family in the Lord.

Right now I am sitting in a passenger waiting lounge in Rome's Leonardo da Vinci airport. Joy is reclining beside me, trying to catch up on the sleep we missed on our flight last night. I can't sleep.

It's not our first visit to Rome. The ambience of the Eternal City penetrates to the center of one's consciousness from the moment one steps onto the jetway of this airport. Immediately the ear is bombarded with the indecipherable cacophonies of languages one almost but not quite recognizes, and the eye beholds every human hue and form, costumed with stunning variety. In this cosmopolitan arena, one can't help smiling at God's delicious range of tastes in friendships. He could have been a little more selective; wouldn't it have been simple to invent one perfect mold and stick with it? For whatever reason, that obviously wasn't His choice. He seems intent on exploring an infinity of human possibilities, making this little adjustment and taking in that little tuck so that no two of these teeming *homo sapiens* look or sound exactly alike. In this place, one can't think of an abstract category called "man." Each person appears to be a category of one, too different from the others to be lumped together. Instead, every one seems specially crafted, singular, the object of God's creative affection.

At the moment, the minds of these rushing individuals don't seem to be very much on God. They, like us, are peering anxiously at the video screen, hoping to find their flight announced, hoping it'll be on time, hoping it won't be canceled. We're in the transit section; we've all come from someplace and are going someplace else. We can't leave this area without passing through passport control. For the time being, we're in international no-man's land. We don't really belong here. We're all aliens and sojourners, not friends, related only by the circumstances of our travels, strangers passing briefly on our way to somewhere else. We make idle conversation, complain about the humidity and the airline service and the inconveniences, not meaning anything by it—just passing time.

We are not merely strangers, though. We are strangers only to one another. Elsewhere we are friends.

The polite man at the ticket counter has just smilingly informed us that our flight has been delayed two more hours. We try to return his smile. He won't get many. That makes eleven hours we will have been sitting here—if we aren't delayed again. Our thoughts turn longingly to the East. Just one more link in this journey and we'll be in India. My mind is thinking of the dear ones we met there thirteen years ago. Some of them we'll be able to see again this time; others we'll miss because our time is too brief.

For an American, India is an exotic land of strange sounds and mystifying religions and frightening poverty. We haven't forgotten our culture shock on our first journey there. We couldn't take it all in. We won't this time, either. We are steeling ourselves for what we'll see.

Our memories aren't limited to the surprises, though. We are going back thirteen years later because we gratefully recall the Christians we dwelt among in those few brief weeks. We have not been able to forget them, the kindness in their faces, the generosity of their hospitality. We became friends. It'll be a happy reunion.

Even as we are thinking forward, our hearts turn homeward as well. We left our grown children back there in the States, and our parents and the rest of our biological family. We smile inwardly as we recall them and breathe our prayers for God's protection for them. There are others, too, many others, in our prayers. I am tempted to list them for you here, as Paul so often mentions his friends by name. (See Romans 16:1-15, for example.) Our list would be long. You wouldn't recognize most of their names; we wish you would. We'd love for you to know them. They are special; they are our friends. They are Christ's friends.

They are therefore infinitely important. I guess that's what this chapter is really about and what gives such urgency to His commission. He's concerned about His friends, those already enjoying the protection and fellowship of His body and those still outside. They are all God's individual creatures, to be cherished for their own sake, no matter what the ideologies of men may teach to the contrary.

In one of his books, German theologian Helmut Thielicke writes of the time he buried a young father suddenly felled by disease. His fellow Nazis attended the funeral, storm troopers, other administrators, district leaders, and party propaganda functionaries. They stood impatiently about the grave, unsympathetic with anything a God-believing preacher would have to say.

Thielicke didn't flinch before their hostility. Instead, he attacked their atheistic philosophy at its root. They may protest that man is "only a leaf on the tree of the nation," but he dared them to call this particular man, this father of his children and husband of this widow, merely a leaf, a part that can easily be replaced by another part. Of course, his functions can be taken up by another, but he himself is irreplaceable.

> Before God every man is infinitely precious, for Jesus Christ died for every man. And now you can judge for yourselves who is right: God, who considers his people precious and for whom none is too insignificant; or those men, who see in another man only the bearer of a function and accordingly consider him replaceable, who think of him as being only a blighted leaf.[1]

Think of your friends, as I am thinking of mine. Which one is "replaceable"? Which one is not unique, special? Which one is a mere "blighted leaf"? Which one does not matter to God?

It's too bad, isn't it, that Jesus' final instructions have become the object of so much theological attention we always speak of them in capital letters? THE GREAT COMMISSION. The importance of the words deserve this respect, but our reverence for them misleads us. What is Jesus really thinking here, if not of His love for His friends, every one of them, in every place. Each one is special. None is to be dismissed as a mere leaf, a replaceable part, a passing phenomenon.

The Good Shepherd knows His sheep by name.

So does the Good Friend know His friends by name.

And the Good Friend knows that, in spite of our uniqueness, we hold some things in common. Most obviously, we all need Him. So Jesus urges His disciples to pass the blessings they have received to as many people as they can possibly get to: "Make disciples, baptizing them in the name of the Father and the Son and the Holy Spirit, and teaching them to observe all that I have commanded you."

No exceptions here. All the world needs discipleship. All the world needs to be baptized into followership; all the world needs to be taught the truths Jesus has revealed; all the world needs friendship with Jesus. All the world!

We must not miss something else about Jesus' concern for all His friends. He cares for them in every place and in every era. His love knows boundaries of neither space nor time. "And surely I am with you always, to the very end of the age." So convinced is Peter of Jesus' universal love, on the Day of Pentecost he announces the vast extent of God's gospel offer: "The promise is for you and your children *and for all who are far off* —for all whom the Lord our God will call" (Acts 2:39). His disciples know His voice. They hear Him saying still:

"I am with you now, as you leave this place and begin your ministry."

"I am with you even when you cannot see me or touch me or hear my voice."

"I am with you whenever two or three of you are gathered together in My name."

"I am with you even when I seem to be dead."

"I am with you even when you seem to be dead."

"I am with you in time and in eternity, in the here and now and in the there and then."

"I am with you because you are My friends. I am with you as you help My other friends."

"I am with you as long as this age exists, and longer."

"I am with you as long as you exist.

"I am with you."

This promise means that as Joy and I prepare to board the plane for India, we can anticipate a glad reunion there with His friends and ours. It means that in subsequent journeys to distant lands, when we arrive, we shall fall into the loving hands of Jesus' friends. Later, when we embark on the journey to our final destination, we can anticipate another, endless, glad reunion with His friends and ours. Jesus' friendships reach around the world and through time to eternity.

He is with us, all of us, everywhere, forever.

He is the ultimate friend.

---

[1]Helmut Thielicke, *The Freedom of the Christian Man: A Christian Confrontation with the Secular Gods* (Grand Rapids: Baker, 1963), pp. 212, 213.

CHAPTER TEN

Tough and Tender Friendship

2 Timothy 1:16; 2 Timothy 4:9

I haven't heard from a former correspondent for several months now. I may never hear again. If I don't, it'll be my own fault.

We have been writing one another for many years. Ours has not been an easy correspondence, at least for me, although it has been beneficial. My pen pal possesses one of the finest minds I know. His wit is dangerously sharp and, when honed on the strop of his divers prejudices, cuts and slashes whoever stands in its way, which is just about everybody.

That is why our correspondence has stopped. As I said, it's my fault. One day something in me snapped; I suddenly became intolerant of his intolerance. So many of my friends have fallen before his stinging rebukes, so much of what I am doing and what I stand for has been abruptly dismissed as unworthy of my calling, I ran out of defenses. We're both guilty of violating a maxim of friendship: "If you want to win friends, you have to learn to lose arguments." Neither one of us has been a very good loser.

We erstwhile academicians would profit from a review of Ralph Waldo Emerson's classic essay on friendship. He diagnoses what is missing in our exchanges. According to Emerson,

> there are two elements that go to the composition of friendship, each so sovereign that I can detect no superiority in either, no reason why either should be first named. One is Truth. A friend is a person with whom I may be sincere. Before him I may think aloud.... Every man alone is sincere. At the entrance of a second person, hypocrisy begins. We parry and fend the approach of our fellow man by compliments, by gossip, by amusements,

by affairs. We cover up our thought from him under a hundred folds. . . .

The other element of friendship is Tenderness. We are holden to men by every sort of tie, by blood, by pride, by fear, by hope, by lucre, by lust, by hate, by admiration, by every circumstance and badge and trifle, but we can scarce believe that so much character can subsist in another as to draw us by love. Can another be so blessed and we so pure that we can offer him tenderness?[1]

There you have it. My correspondent and I have been writing to one another with admirable candor, but without the requisite tenderness. He is no more at fault than I. We have been proud of our intellectual integrity, enjoining the no-holds-barred repartee that we learned in undergraduate college, but we have been only half-persons to each other, avidly exploring the hidden crevices of our mental storehouses while ignoring that we are total persons, with feelings and associations and hurts and painful memories and insecurities we don't want to admit but aren't successful in camouflaging. We've tried to be tough. We haven't been tender. In time, our sensitivities have been pricked sore by piercing truths and sharp retorts. Tough isn't enough by itself. Tender, even among men, is wanted. The ego is fragile.

Since so many of life's exchanges are bruising ones, we retreat hungrily to the company of a friend who permits us to expose a bit of our wounded psyche without pouncing on it. Our toughness has so often been met with toughness that we generally fear our tenderness will be met with scorn. So we usually remain tough, slugging it out to avoid having to reveal our inner selves that crave tenderness. But to that special friend, whom we know will not strike us down, we can open up. We know we'll be met with tenderness. The incisive Victorian author George Eliot (is there any significance in my returning so frequently to earlier centuries to learn about friendship?) puts it this way:

Oh, the inexpressible comfort of feeling safe with a person; having neither to weigh thoughts nor measure words, but to pour them all out, just as they are, chaff and grain together, knowing that a faithful hand will take and sift them, keep what is worth keeping, and then, with the breath of kindness, blow the rest away.[2]

It's that kindness that we seek, perhaps even more than we seek the truth. We yearn for someone who, while not disregarding our more obvious qualities, cares enough to find the hidden ones. I have had the privilege of working for nearly a decade with a man considerably younger than I am who has demonstrated that ability. For many years he was our youth minister. In that role, he quietly and steadily helped our young people develop their potential. Early in my ministry here, another friend visited us on a Sunday, volunteered his opinions on the church's strengths and weakness, and among his unsolicited recommendations he advised me to replace our youth minister with a more "dynamic" man. I ignored his advice. It would have been a terrible thing to do. My adviser hastily drew the wrong conclusions on the basis of one morning's observations. (How often, on so many subjects, are we wrong because our look is too fleeting, too shallow?) He had no way of knowing what the rest of us were learning about Steve's gifts. His greatest strength was in his patient tutoring, his ability to spot hidden virtue and nurture it to maturity. He wasn't "dynamic" if you limit the term to refer to the charismatic platform personality; he created a dynamic youth group, however, by touching off the dynamite in the personalities of his kids. He cared enough to find and accentuate their best.

Keith Miller tells an unforgettable story on himself in his book, *Habitation of Dragons*. A counselor in a boys' camp after his freshman year in college, he was in charge of a cabin full of junior boys eight and nine years old. One of the boys drew especially close to him. Mortey was an orphan; he quickly adopted Keith as his dad during the week. At the same time, he enjoyed genuine popularity with his peers because of his sense of humor, intelligence, and leadership ability. He also impressed the counselors. Mortey was one of two boys who remained in the race for junior honor camper. Feeling too biased to vote, Keith abstained, but when the ballots were counted, a tie was declared. Keith had to break the tie.

Again determined to show no partiality, Keith did his best to be objective. Both boys had strengths: Bobby was the better

117

athlete, Mortey the expert in human relations. Keith knew Mortey better, of course, and he had seen some of Mortey's weaknesses. He *was* a little cocky, perhaps. Keith voted for Bobby.

Then he felt miserable. He had been honest, but he couldn't feel right about his decision. He needed to talk to Mortey, to level with him about why he had voted against him. So on the last morning of the camp, when Mortey came up to say good-bye, Keith saw the tears he was trying to hide. They walked away from the rest of the boys so Keith could tell him what their friendship had meant to him. He told him about the tie vote and how, in order to preserve his integrity, he had voted for Bobby. He started to explain, but he couldn't go on. The horrified look on Mortey's face stopped him.

> In an instant I saw how wrong I had been and why. This little boy really loved me. And I realized that he had done a much finer job than Bobby at camp. But because Mortey had loved me, he had revealed his faults as well as his good points to me, and I had used this knowledge to judge and condemn him (from his perspective).[3]

Mortey stared in disbelief. His father had let him down by leaving the family; in place of his father, he had trusted Keith. And now another rejection. He ran away and hid on the bus. Mortey was gone. Forever.

Keith had done the principled thing. He had protected his integrity. He could congratulate himself on his virtue. He had been tough, but his little friend needed tenderness.

They are opposites, these virtues, opposites that friends must hold together. We need to hear the tough truths, but the truth we long to hear most of all is that we are accepted, approved, wanted—special, to somebody! Miller concludes that there is something more important, more virtuous, than what he calls "raw honesty." It's called love.

"Tough Love" has become a popular catch phrase in recent years. There's even an organization for frazzled parents by this name. I applaud its philosophy. More than that, I subscribe to it, but with one proviso: love must never be so tough it calluses its tenderness. It must not cease to care, to sense, to be tactful. It cannot demand conformity on every point to its standards and beliefs; it should never lose its ability to see through eyes other than its own. Love that is tough without tenderness in the end is not love at all.

This is not the easiest lesson for Christians. Some conservative and fundamentalist circles, especially, insist that we exclude from fellowship all whose doctrine differs from the "true faith." Convinced they have the corner on the truth, they fear lest too much social intercourse with those who think differently will somehow contaminate them. So they toughly demand conformity to their convictions since theirs, they verily believe, conform precisely to what the Lord expects.

How these untainted disciples are supposed to "go into all the nations and make disciples" if they cannot befriend those who differ they don't make clear. How this satisfies Jesus' prayer for the unity of His believers is another unanswered question. Still another is how Christians can love one another while withholding tenderness.

Many Bible readers are put off by the toughness of God's justice. My own reading of it just as frequently impresses me with His tenderness. Jesus' picture of God in the story of the Prodigal Son (Luke 15) is the one I carry close to my heart. It gives this prodigal hope. While Jesus never leads us to expect less than justice from God, He encourages us to hope for more, for His grace and mercy. Since we are saved by His tender mercies, it behooves us to treat one another with the same mercy.

Another picture I carry in my heart is the one of His family. The Bible calls us God's chosen people, His household. Have you looked at them very carefully? Can't you hear God saying in the beginning to those Israelites Moses was dragging out of captivity in Egypt to their promised land, "You—yes you— you are My people. I chose you a long time ago when I called your father Abraham and promised to make him a great nation. I blessed him and I blessed his son Isaac and Isaac's son Jacob. I haven't forgotten you even in Egypt. Now I am leading you to freedom.

"Why am I doing this for you? You know it doesn't really have much to do with your inherent virtue. You're not much different from the people from whom I'm setting you free. What makes you a 'peculiar people' is My love for you. Sometimes you exasperate Me, you with your incessant whining and fickleness. Even when you protest that you love Me back, your efforts to convince Me are pretty feeble. I've caught you lying and cheating and fornicating and in every imaginable way forsaking Me. Sometimes I've had to discipline you pretty severely. But there is one lesson I want you to learn and learn well: you are My people. I love you. I care about you. I will not forsake you. More than that, I will do everything I can to rescue you from your enemies and yourself and to bring to you and out of you the best there is."

Tough—and oh so tender.

On the pages of the New Testament, God is still calling a mixed bag of characters into His family. We could turn almost at random and find examples of their peculiar diversity, their comforting ordinariness, an unoutstandingness so much like our own, giving us cause to believe there might be room in the family for the likes of us. I've chosen 2 Timothy 4:9-22, which lists a typical mix of saints and sinners among the friends of God.

First the saints.

Titus

The son of Gentile parents, Titus accompanied Paul to Jerusalem. His non-Jewish blood gave Paul an opportunity to strike a blow for the principle of accepting Gentiles into the church on the basis of faith in Christ only, without their having to subscribe to the law (Galatians 2:3). Titus later became a strong leader. During Paul's third missionary journey, he assigned Titus to Corinth to solve its problems and to assist with the Jerusalem offering. Later he went to Crete to organize its churches.

Titus, an easy man to befriend.

Luke

Undoubtedly acting at times as personal physician to the aging, often ailing apostle, Luke frequently accompanied Paul. He was a Gentile convert to the Christian faith. Well educated, Luke has enriched all subsequent Christian history through the Gospel of Luke and the book of Acts. Luke must have been a warm person, for he was called "the beloved" (dear friend) in Colossians 4:14.

Luke, undoubtedly the most notable personality in this list.

Mark

There was a time when Paul wanted little to do with this young man (Acts 15:36-39). Now he calls for him. Here is a friendship that survived "in spite of. . . ."

The home of Mark's mother seems to have been the central meeting place of the Jerusalem church, so Mark enjoyed being in the inner circle of Christian leaders from the beginning. (Did he also glory in being so young a companion of these more experienced leaders?) Mark was a natural companion for Saul (later Paul) and Barnabas on their first missionary journey (Acts 13:5). He was a young man with a future, but suddenly he had no future, at least with Paul.

The missionaries first evangelized the island of Cyprus, but when they reached Perga in Pamphylia, Mark returned abruptly to Jerusalem. We aren't certain why. Homesickness maybe, or fear of the rugged journey ahead, or even perhaps disappointment that Paul was emerging as leader ahead of Mark's friend and relative Barnabas. Whatever Mark's motive, Paul refused to take him along on his next journey.

When we next hear of Mark, however, he appears in Rome, where he is a fellow worker with Paul (Philemon 24), who later recommends him to the church at Colosse (Colossians 4:10). The friendship recovered. Paul's toughness softened enough to allow reconciliation with the younger man.

Tychicus

We know little of this man, but everything we know is good. Probably a native of Ephesus, this man held the affection and confidence of Paul and the rest of the Christians, as demonstrated by his work as trusted courier of letters and money between bodies of Christians (2 Corinthians 8:19) and as Paul's faithful companion during his imprisonment.

Priscilla and Aquila

This couple must not be omitted. These itinerant tentmakers appear in Corinth (Acts 18:2), Ephesus (Acts 18:24-26, 1 Corinthians 16:19), and Rome (Romans 16:3). Everywhere they go, they become active leaders in the church, teaching and serving with boldness and tenderness. Paul says in Romans 16:3 and 4 that "all the churches of the Gentiles are grateful to them."

Onesiphorus

This is the one who started my thinking about tough, tender friends in the Lord. He is just mentioned here, but in 2 Timothy 1:16, Paul writes, "May the Lord show mercy to the household of Onesiphorus, because he often refreshed me and was not ashamed of my chains." Onesiphorus exemplifies the kind of friendship we are discussing. He courageously joined ranks with the unpopular prisoner, undoubtedly at some personal risk. This boldness triggered my whole chain of thoughts about the extent to which friends go in accepting each other in spite of their imperfections, their mixed motives, their uncomfortable or threatening circumstances. Paul, even out of prison, could not have been an easy friend. His mercurial temperament, his intensity, his stubbornly held convictions, and his single-minded pursuit of his calling had to make him something less than a comfortable companion. Then there was his propensity for offending the "movers and shakers" of every town he entered. Friendship with Paul required large heaps of tolerance, a quality Onesiphorus had in abundance.

Trophimus

Here is another who must not be omitted because of the trouble he got his friend Paul into. A Gentile Christian of Ephesus (Acts 21:29), Trophimus also helped carry the collection to Jerusalem, where hostile Asian Jews jumped to the erroneous conclusion that Paul had illegally introduced him into the temple itself (Acts 21:29). (Who hasn't sometime been in trouble because of his companions?)

From these good and faithful friends, we turn to the problem personalities in the lineup.

Demas

Demas "loved this world" enough to desert Paul. He had been a faithful helper of Paul during his imprisonment in Rome (Colossians 4:14). (Paul calls him a "fellow laborer" in Philemon 24.) Then he bailed out. We wonder why. Did he sign up without counting the cost? Did he just wear out? Did he become disillusioned?

Alexander the Metalworker

This man did Paul "a great deal of harm." The apostle turned him over to the Lord ("The Lord will repay him for what he has done") and warned his fellow Christians about him: "You too should be on your guard against him, because he strongly opposed our message." We don't know anything more about him. What did he do to Paul? Was he responsible for his arrest? Was he an informer?

You cannot read this list of names without concluding that, even in Paul's relatively small circle of fellow workers, all kinds were included. Some proved themselves sterling, others straw. Friends as diverse as these or as those original disciples of Jesus cannot long stay together without generous amounts of tough and tender love.

As God befriended an often offending Israel, as Jesus drew to himself unfinished and misunderstanding disciples, so the church through the ages has opened its doors to every expression of humanity and has befriended them with a love at once tough and tender.

Years ago, the bulletin of City Temple Church in London included this announcement:

> To all who are weary and seek rest; to all who mourn and long for comfort; to all who struggle and desire victory; to all who sin and need a savior; to all who are idle and look for service; to all who are strangers and want fellowship; to all who hunger and thirst after righteousness; and to whosoever will come—this church opens wide her doors and offers her welcome in the name of Jesus Christ her Lord.

It's a blanket invitation to friendship in the name of Jesus. If the church really meant these words, and if they were accepted, a motley of mankind must have made up the fellowship there. Tolerance could not be optional.

St. Stephen's Walbrook, another London church, worded the invitation as a prayer:

> O God, make the door of this house wide enough to receive all who need human love and fellowship; narrow enough to shut out all envy, pride and strife.

Make its threshold smooth enough to be no stumbling block to children, nor straying feet, but rugged and strong enough to turn back the tempter's power. God, make the door of this house the gateway to thine eternal kingdom.

I have quoted these churchly invitations because it has been as a minister of the church that I have come to understand that love—and, therefore, friendship—consists of toughness and tenderness and tolerance, tolerance both tough and tender. The church must be tough; its standards are exacting and its devotion to truth undeviating. But the church is also, of all organizations I know anything about, the most tolerant. It accepts anybody. In the name of Jesus, it forgives anybody. It patiently, lovingly, gently, mercifully, and carefully imitates the ministry of Jesus among His unworthy disciples, nurturing them with His unerring balance of toughness and tenderness as He called them into His circle of friends, taught them the truth, disciplined them when they strayed from it, and waited for them to grow up into full maturity. While He waited, He loved them anyway. It's what tough and tender friendship does.

---

[1]Ralph Waldo Emerson, "Friendship," Charles W. Eliot, ed., *The Harvard Classics: The Five-Foot Shelf of Books*, Volume 5 (New York: P.F. Collier and Son, 1909), pp. 115, 116.

[2]Quoted in *Leadership*, Winter, 1988, p. 112.

[3]Keith Miller, *Habitation of Dragons* (Waco: Word, 1970), pp. 20-24.

CHAPTER ELEVEN

Friends of the Moment

Luke 23:12

I loved my friend.
He went away from me.
There's nothing more to say.
The poem ends,
Soft as it began—
I loved my friend.[1]

During the 1988 Presidential campaign, the newspaper carried an analysis of the two current leading candidates. One was presented as a popular man who enjoyed the company of a host of friends, convivial but perhaps excessively loyal to his companions, who might hold too much sway over him. This trait could cause him to be an insufficiently independent leader. In contrast, his opponent apparently felt no compunction in abruptly cutting off any friend who stood in the way of reaching his objectives. It isn't that he didn't have friends, the article explained, but they were friends of the moment, comrades in a common cause. So long as a person was forwarding the cause, friendship with the candidate was possible; when he became a liability, he had to go.

As you can tell, I haven't been able to put this article out of my mind. I wondered whether I could vote for a man who considered his friends expendable, like any other useful commodity. There seemed something too cold, too calculating, even too inhuman in such an attitude.

Not long before, I had been reading some books about Russia's *refuseniks*, those battered, suffering Jews who have endured every conceivable indignity because they dared to apply for exit visas for Israel or some other country. In one book, Mark Ya. Abzel[2] contrasts Stalin and Hitler. He takes issue with people who find them equally monstrous.

125

Hitler was a monster mainly toward other peoples; but Stalin was a monster toward his own people. He destroyed his loyal friends, his allies, his benefactors, as ruthlessly as he did his enemies; laid waste to the wealth and sustenance of the nation he ruled.

When his countrymen stood between him and whatever he wanted, even his closest comrades fell before his wrath. Millions of peasants never had a chance.

This is exactly what so horrifies us about King Herod in the Christmas story, isn't it? How could he have turned against the innocents? Was there no limit to the man's depravity?

Back to the presidential campaign. My comparing the candidate with such historical ogres as Hitler, Stalin, and Herod may strike you as farfetched, but I am wondering whether there is much difference, except in degree, between an office-seeker who will axe his friends to win an election and a tyrant who will destroy his own people to protect his throne. Friends are not means to an end; they are the end.

Herod and Pilate

Provisional friendships are not uncommon, of course. A common cause can bring together persons who otherwise would never choose to be companions. ("Politics makes strange bedfellows.") A classic example of these temporary alliances is recorded in Luke 23:12. "That day Herod and Pilate became friends—before this they had been enemies."

The two rulers had the same problem: Jesus. What should they do with this alleged disturber of the peace? Pilate and Herod (not Herod the Great of the Christmas story, but his son Herod the Tetrarch) were rivals, vying with each other for Rome's favor. Under ordinary circumstances, no love was lost between them. Yet here, for this moment, Luke calls them "friends," a common if overly generous misuse of the term. Luke writes with intended irony; he has just painted a picture of the perverse pleasure the king took in insulting the Galilean:

Then Herod and his soldiers ridiculed and mocked him. Dressing him in an elegant robe, they sent him back to Pilate. That day Herod and Pilate became friends. . . .

Not friends, really. Their alliance won't last. Joined for the moment in their political dilemma (neither of them wanting to handle Jesus' potentially explosive case), enjoying a bit of fun at His expense, for once having a common enemy instead of being antagonists, they feel kindly affectioned toward one another. For the moment. They will like each other as long as their accord is mutually useful. When it no longer serves their purposes, one will drop the other without remorse.

This is one of the reasons, the least commendable one, for the old complaint of leaders that it's lonely at the top. Loneliness is guaranteed to anyone who chooses friends on the basis of their usefulness. A solitary life, even one surrounded by people, is guaranteed when you use your friends to get what you want, manipulate your relationships to your own advantage, strike a bargain with anybody who will help you get what you desire and then, when you have everything arranged to your profit, get rid of your "friends" and enjoy your booty.

Judas and Jesus

Judas employed the strategy to perfection. Although we aren't really certain what caused Judas to betray his Friend, many Bible students believe it was because Judas, a super-patriot, became disillusioned. He had hoped Jesus would lead His troops in an insurrection against their Roman overlords. It was time for action; the Jews deserved to be free. In the beginning, Judas saw in Jesus the makings of a great charismatic revolutionary, so he signed on. With time, however, Judas became increasingly convinced that this proclaimer of a peaceable kingdom would rather suffer than inflict suffering; the kingdom of which He spoke would not supplant Rome. He was not a man of action after all. In dismay, the desperate Judas gave up on Him and, practical (or should we say greedy) to the end, he recovered what he could from his years of service (thirty pieces of silver). At least he didn't suffer a total loss!

He did it with a kiss. The sign of friendship.

Earlier, he had compounded his treachery by accepting Jesus' hospitality at the Last Supper. Jesus, knowing what was in Judas's heart, offered him this final symbol of His acceptance and love. Hypocritically, Judas took what was offered, took it and fled. Was it because, as has been suggested, his loss of confidence in Jesus was now complete? Had Judas concluded there was no way he would get what he wanted through this man, so he must turn to somebody else? Or was it something less political, more personal—like fear for his life? The disciples all discerned the mortal danger into which Jesus was going in Jerusalem. His enemies had long been plotting against Him. Now they would strike. Maybe Judas was just trying to escape with his skin—and take a little money along with him.

Whatever the reason, he sold out his Friend and sought his own advantage in the transaction: "What are you willing to give me if I hand him over to you?" (Matthew 26:15). He grabbed his silver and watched for his opportunity.

For this singular deed, the great poet Dante consigned him to the very innermost core of Hell. Dante's inspired imagination couldn't conceive of anyone or anything worse in history than this fiendish betrayer of our Lord. On a much more personal level, is there anything worse we can imagine than to have a trusted friend turn against us?

But what right do we have to believe the same thing won't happen to us? Or that we won't do the same? When friends are a means to an end, and when the end is getting what we want, then is there any limit to the extent we will go to get it?

A few years ago, there was a documentary on television that had been filmed in Newark and New York City. Parental discretion was advised for viewing the program, which was about what a lack of parental discretion had created. The camera stared remorselessly at every form of violence: bloodied heads and "stoned" madmen—all of them teenagers. In an unforgettable exchange, producer-director Helen Whitney asked, "Where do you draw the line at violence?" The adolescent sulked, "Ain't no limit. If I gotta kill you to get what I want, I'll kill you." Thus Judas.

This altogether-too-pervasive attitude is what makes it so frightening to be living in an era that glamorizes hedonism, that teaches impressionable young people it is necessary and commendable to go for what they want and let nothing stand in the way. Even friendship.

It's the same bad advice that Shakespeare's Polonius gives his son Horatio in *Hamlet*:

To thine own self be true,
And it must follow, as the night the day,
Thou can'st not then be false to any man.

Polonius is simply not telling the truth. You can be false if the self you are true to is rotten. Greedy persons are always true to themselves. So are the manipulators who are forever arranging things and rearranging people to their own advantage. They will get what they want no matter what it takes. If you get hurt in the process, tough. If you should complain, who will listen? They're merely being true to themselves.

They're like another of Shakespeare's characters, Richard III. As Shakespeare presents him, the Duke of Gloucester (before usurping the throne) soberly surveys his future. His badly misshapen body reflects his equally misshapen soul. Having nothing in his looks to attract a woman, he concludes that he is condemned to live with loneliness. Then, in one of the playwright's psychologically astute insights, he has the future king resolve,

And therefore, since I cannot prove a lover,
To entertain these fair well-spoken days,
I am determined to prove a villain
And hate the idle pleasures of these days.

For better or for worse, he will get what he's after.

Friends of the Moment Aren't Friends at All

The truth is quite plain, isn't it? Men and women who live by manipulation cannot, in the end, be friends. You can't trust them in anything except what is to their own advantage. This is not a new discovery. Some of our oldest Scriptures lament the loss of fair-weather friends. Here is Jeremiah's description of Jerusalem in the day of her destruction. He pictures her as a woman who has lost her last friends. To be bereft of friends is the essence of desolation.

Bitterly she weeps at night,
   tears are upon her cheeks.
Among all her lovers
   there is none to comfort her.

> All her friends have betrayed her;
>> they have become her enemies (Lamentations 1:2).

Erstwhile friends have turned against her; even the leaders who should have felt responsible, if not compassionate, ignore her as they scramble to take care of themselves:

> I called to my allies
>> but they betrayed me.
> My priests and my elders
>> perished in the city
> while they searched for food
>> to keep themselves alive (Lamentations 1:19).

Jeremiah speaks from personal experience. So does the Lord. And for those of use who have experienced the same, how true His words ring in our ears:

> "Beware of your friends;
>> do not trust your brothers.
> For every brother is a deceiver,
>> and every friend a slanderer.
> Friend deceives friend,
>> and no one speaks the truth.
> They have taught their tongues to lie;
>> they weary themselves with sinning.
> You live in the midst of deception;
>> in their deceit they refuse to acknowledge me," declares the
>> Lord (Jeremiah 9:4, 5).

Even some of the Psalms are laments. This one ascribed to David (Psalm 55:12-14) is especially poignant:

> If an enemy were insulting me,
>> I could endure it;
> if a foe were raising himself against me,
>> I could hide from him.
> But it is you, a man like myself,
>> my companion, my close friend,
> with whom I once enjoyed sweet fellowship
>> as we walked with the throng at the house of God.

The experience these lines depict is so universal one could be tempted to wonder whether real friendship is ever possible. If so, with whom? Who is trustworthy enough to be a friend? On whom can one count in the day of trouble?

Jesus and Judas Revisited

We need to return to the Last Supper and look again at what is transpiring between Jesus and Judas. Above, we concentrated on Judas. That is enough to discourage anyone. For three years, Jesus has poured himself into these disciples but, in Judas's case, without profit. This man who has studied His teachings, enjoyed His fellowship, accepted His hospitality, allowed Him to wash his feet, and in every other way received blessings from the Master, returns the favors with betrayal and death. How can friendship with such a person be possible?

It can't, really. How can you trust yourself to a person who is all take and no give?

But if we despair of ever having a mutually trustworthy friendship, it is because we are studying the wrong person. Look at Jesus: in spite of what He knows of Judas's frailties, He keeps on giving to him. He does not allow Judas's weakness to dilute His own strength. Because there is one betrayer in the crowd, Jesus does not withhold friendship—either from him or from the other eleven. Yes, Jesus will be betrayed, but not by all of them. Yes, the rest will disappoint Him in His hour of greatest need, but not forever. They may, in their panic, fail to act as friends should, but He does not renounce friendship itself or even give up on these particular friends. They may waver, but He won't.

As loyal as Judas is disloyal, Jesus treats them all to dinner and, as the meal is being served, He takes towel and wash basin in hand to wash their feet. He will serve them though they desert him. With the common cup and loaf, He infuses the morrow's events with eternal meaning. "This is my body . . . for you." "This is my blood . . . for you." My friendship is forever. Even though you will prove untrustworthy in my hour of trial, you can trust Me. Always. In spite of everything.

Jesus and Peter

If any doubt should linger about the unconditional quality of Jesus' friendship, a look at John 21 should dispel it. Peter and half-a-dozen of the other disciples have spent the night fishing, but without success. Early in the morning, Jesus, standing on the shore, spots their boat and calls out to them.

"Friends, haven't you any fish?" (John 21:5).

Before writing this book, I had never paid any attention to Jesus' greeting here. I can't think of any other occasion, though, when Jesus greets His disciples this way. It is another instance, a small one admittedly, of Jesus' several postresurrection attempts to repair the breach opened by His disciples' betrayal, denial, and withdrawal from Him. Think of the guilt they must have felt. In their guilt, they reacted predictably. When we feel we have wronged someone, our natural inclination is to avoid the one we have wronged. In every occasion of these appearances of Jesus, He takes the initiative to effect a reconciliation: He reassures the grieving women at the tomb; He reconfirms the disciples' commission; He offers proof to the doubting Thomas; He invites them to eat with Him (thus keeping the promise He made to them at the Last Supper). His special concern, though, is Peter. Of the remaining disciples (Judas by this time has already killed himself), Peter feels he has fallen the furthest. He needs a double portion of grace, of reassurance. When the angel at the tomb tells the women to ask the disciples to meet Jesus in Galilee, he singles out Peter. The Lord wants him to know that he, especially, is welcome again in His circle of intimates.

The most moving scene of reconciliation takes place along the shore after Jesus has helped His friends find their extraordinary catch. Following a meal, Jesus leads Peter through this personal ritual of reconciliation.

> "Simon son of John, do you truly love me more than these?"
> "Yes, Lord, you know that I love you."
> "Feed my lambs. . . .
> "Simon, son of John, do you truly love me?"
> "Yes, Lord, you know that I love you."
> "Take care of my sheep. . . .
> "Simon son of John, do you love me?"
> At this third asking, Peter's feelings are hurt. Why does Jesus persist? "Lord, you know all things; you know that I love you." "Feed my sheep." Then, after a little explanation, Jesus simply adds, "Follow me." (See John 21:15-19.)

Three times Peter had denied his Lord; now his Lord gives him three opportunities to wipe away the denials. This time, though, Jesus insists that words won't be enough. He must follow. He must obey. He must take care of the dependent ones Jesus is leaving behind.

In Jesus' hour of trial, Peter's friendship proved untrue. But Jesus' friendship has never wavered. He wants His friend Peter to be with Him now. For sure.

Forever.

Trustworthiness—the Mark of a Friend

This chapter has been about trustworthiness. It agrees with the Chinese proverb: "Mutual confidence is the pillar of friendship." Peter Ustinov somewhat cynically alludes to this quality in his autobiography.

> I do not believe that friends are necessarily the people you like best, they are merely the people who got there first. . . . You are stuck with most of them for life . . . often with people who are entirely reprehensible, unreliable, and even spiteful.[3]

You are only stuck with them, though, if you want to be. As we noted earlier, there are ways to get rid of them, if that's what you want. If you are an otherwise trustworthy person, however, your character won't easily let you shake off your friends, even when they let you down. Jesus couldn't really dismiss Peter from His circle, although most people would not have blamed Him for doing so. Even though Peter was still too immature to be able to extend true friendship, Jesus wasn't. As the more mature of the two, He could forgive and wait for the still-growing Peter.

Paul Johnson tells a story every reader of this book (and certainly the writer) can identify with. He says it was in the fourth grade that he learned this valuable lesson about trustworthiness.

One day he found fifty cents, somebody else's lunch money. Miss Argabright asked the class if anyone had found it. Everybody, including Paul, denied seeing it. She then went around the room to ask every pupil to whisper in her ear if he or she had it. Paul confessed and at the next recess returned the fifty cents to the teacher's desk.

Three weeks later, someone apparently rammed a pencil into the mouth of a pet turtle and left it bleeding from the wound. Again, the class was questioned and again no one admitted to the deed. This time Miss Argabright asked each pupil to come alone to her office. When Paul, who wouldn't have hurt either his teacher or the turtle, protested his innocence, she said, "A few weeks ago you lied to me, how do I know you are not lying now? You were one of the students who was playing with the turtle, and I think perhaps you did it."

Young Paul told this story on himself many years later as a mature adult. It taught him, he said,

> the importance of having a friend convinced that I was telling the truth. Religion and ethics may be difficult to teach, but Miss Argabright taught me, at an early age, that the loss of a friend's trust leaves one defenseless.[4]

And, we must add, friendless.

"Therefore," as Paul writes in Ephesians 4:25, "each of you must put off falsehood and speak truthfully to his neighbor, for we are all members of one body."

Otherwise, the only friends you can have will be friends of the moment.

---

[1]Langston Hughes, *The Dream Keeper and Other Poems* (©1932, 1960 by Langston Hughes). Used by permission of Alfred A. Knopf, Inc.

[2]Mark Ya. Abzel, *Refusenik* (London: Hamish Hamilton, 1981), p. 11.

[3]Peter Ustinov, *Dear Me* (New York: Atlantic Monthly, 1977). Quoted in *Saturday Review* (September 3, 1977), p. 33.

[4]Paul E. Johnson, *Healer of the Mind* (Nashville: Abingdon, 1972), pp. 182, 183.

CHAPTER TWELVE

Can't We Still Be Friends?
Ecclesiastes 4:9-12

As a girl, the young woman had been very close to her family. But, after graduating from high school, she abruptly broke away, insisting she had "to do my own thing." Her adopted life-style grieved her parents. As the chasm between her and the rest of the family deepened, she stubbornly rejected her parents' values while just as stubbornly trying to retain her place in the family circle.

On the telephone one evening, she asked her mother, "Can't we still be friends?"

Her mother, broken-hearted over her daughter's self-destructive course, disappointed her. "No, we can't," she said. "You can be my daughter and I will always be your mother and love you with a mother's love, but we can't be friends."

The mother, after long nights of soul-searching, was facing a reality her less experienced daughter didn't want to acknowledge. Her parents would hang on to her with all the strength of their love, what the Bible calls "agape," which is love that keeps on loving even when the loved one doesn't deserve or return it. "Agape" love is stronger than friendship. In addition, family ties are reinforced by obligations and expectations that friendship can't call on. These culturally reinforced expectations have given rise to our saying, "Blood is thicker than water." When everyone else lets you down, you can turn to your family. "Home," as Robert Frost has written, "is where when you have to go there, they have to take you in." The girl would never have reason to doubt her mother's love, but the spontaneity, camaraderie, and joy in each other's presence that characterizes intimate friendship was now missing in their relationship. Each was on the defensive, because each felt her value system was being judged and rejected by the other.

I just spoke of "intimate" friendship. Throughout this book, I have often used an adjective to modify the noun, implying there are different levels or types of friendship. The young woman was pleading for her old relationship with the family to be unaffected by her rejection of her parents' beliefs. She had failed to perceive that all people, even parents, not only *have* beliefs, but they *are* what they believe. When you reject someone's beliefs, you lengthen the distance between you.

Is it possible, then, for two people who do not share religious, philosophical, and ethical values to build a lasting friendship? I have asked many people this question lately. Some have answered flatly "no" while others quickly answered "yes." Others had to think a bit about it; without exception, these finally concluded that it wasn't possible. Discussions usually led to the insight that before a definitive answer can be given, we have to be very clear about the kind of friendship we are talking about.

There are at least four levels of friendship: acquaintances, associates, close friends, and intimates. We usually have people we loosely call "friends" at each of these levels. We can love them all. We can love children who violate our standards; we can tolerate acquaintances and associates who walk to the beat of a different drummer; we can even feel pretty close to people of a different religious faith. But we reserve intimacy for those few whom we might call "soul-mates," friends who "know where we are coming from" and are coming from the same place, friends with whom we can be completely ourselves, with our defenses down. Intimate friendship is defenseless.

Because of love's elasticity, we can love someone who does violence to our principles, as the mother would continue to love her wandering daughter. Children elicit this kind of unqualified love from their parents, especially in their adolescent and early adult years. But intimate friendship is more fragile. It asks more of friends. It is also more rewarding.

Acquaintances

The student in August Strindberg's play *The Ghost Sonata* describes much of the human race when he speaks of the man who "was surrounded with a circle of acquaintances; he called them friends for short." A businessman in our community fit the description. When he asked for an appointment, I had no idea what he wanted to talk about. The man seemed to have it all: successful career, generous income, happy family, and a wide circle of friends.

It was this last item he wanted to talk about, though. He was lonely. This popular, outgoing, dynamic man, who knew and was known by so many on a first-name basis, told me, "I don't have a single close friend." Lots of acquaintances, but no friends.

Old Samuel Johnson in the eighteeenth century observed that "if a man does not make new acquaintances, as he advances through life he will soon find himself left alone." I pointed out to the lonely businessman something more obvious to me than to him: he had the promise of many friendships. Anyone who fails to cultivate new acquaintances will indeed end as Dr. Johnson predicts. You see them by the hundreds and thousands, these old people who looked out for themselves when they were younger in every way except this most important of all: they didn't add to their former friends any newer ones. Friendship doesn't begin with intimacy; good friends start out as acquaintances, then they find something in each other's makeup that ignites a desire for a closer relationship, loosely held at first, then more firmly bonded. The businessman had many acquaintances and few friends because he worked more diligently at his career than at his relationships. He had stranded them at the acquaintance level.

Unfortunately, his is not an uncommon plight. Harold Davis, whom I first met nearly a quarter of a century ago when he was the minister of the huge First Christian Church of Canton, Ohio, enjoys telling this delightful story on himself. One Sunday morning, for some reason, he departed from his usual routine and entered the church unexpectedly through the Fourth Street entrance.

"Welcome to our church," the friendly greeter said to him. "We're happy to have you. We have a wonderful minister. You'll enjoy hearing him preach."

To this, the somewhat nonplussed Mr. Davis replied, "I am your minister." Then the greeter was nonplussed.

This man had served as a church greeter for more than thirty years, Harold says. In all that time, he had achieved a distant acquaintanceship with the man behind the pulpit, but he didn't recognize him up close.

I don't mean to sound critical of the faithful servant. One can understand his difficulty. It was a large church building, and from the back it would not be easy to discern Mr. Davis's facial features. He may have had some vision problems as well. I'm repeating the preacher's story because it does fit the circumstances of a good many people I know, including the successful businessman. He knew many people well—at a distance. He had done little, however, to draw any of them closer to himself, to get to know them better. While we all need to be a part of a large circle of acquaintances, we also require something more. Jesus was acquainted with people by the hundreds and thousands, but He called a dozen of them closer, to be His friends. Even He needed them.

This issue has become more complicated since the advent of television. No effort is required for a TV buff to make acquaintances. They are there at the push of a button. People often know more about their favorite television personalities than they do about their next-door neighbors. They are convenient friends to have, dependably there at the same time and same station every week, leading fascinating, often glamorous, lives, guiding the viewer through every range of emotion but never expecting anything in return. Consider the colossal popularity of certain televangelists. They offer their audiences a chance to feel close to their preacher. They make religion enticing and entertaining, even though their world is more than a little bit fantastic. They expose enough of themselves to appear to be offering friendship, of a type. They enter their viewer's (especially their shut-in viewer's) circle of acquaintances.

Our family saw this firsthand a few years ago when we were visiting my father and stepmother. Although they weren't exactly hermits, my parents enjoyed living in a scarcely populated region of the West. Because of uncertain health, they also developed a practice during part of the year of "taking our church at home" by television. On Sunday, they watched from early morning until noon. They felt as if they had been to church. When Rex Humbard came on, Dad pointed out every member of Humbard's family, gave us a little of the history of each personality, and helped us anticipate what would be coming next in the program. It quickly became evident that he knew more about this television family than he did about almost anyone else in his circle of acquaintances.

On another occasion, I was leaving a hospital after making my rounds. I hadn't realized what an important day it was until I overheard the conversation of the three apparently distraught women walking near me. At first, I assumed there must have been a death or other trauma in one of their families, but in a moment I learned the problem. That night was to air the final episode of the Mary Tyler Moore show. They were grieving over a death, all right, the death of Mr. Grant and Ted Baxter and Mary and the rest of the make-believe characters on the popular show. They had all entered these women's circle of acquaintances.

Much has been said and written about the loneliness of contemporary Americans. I'd like to read a little more about television's contribution to this sense of alienation from living people. My guess is that the substituting of television friends for real live ones is taking a terrible psychological toll on unsuspecting addicts. They have impoverished their social lives; they live in Fantasyland and, when forced to deal with flesh and blood persons in the real world, they are unequipped to do so. Dan Rather and Bill Cosby and Cybil Shephard may captivate your attention when they appear on screen, but they are a poor substitute for friends. Go for the real thing. Turn off the television, force yourself out of the house, and circulate. Don't worry if all you accomplish at first is making a few new acquaintances. You will have taken the first step toward friendship.

Associates

The young woman in my study made me feel so unhelpful. A dedicated Christian, a wife, a mother, a faithful worshiper, she had come because she was lonely. "I just can't seem to make any friends," she said. She had tried to befriend this woman and that one, but they apparently didn't want her friendship. At least they didn't return her overtures. What advice could I give her?

139

I made a few feeble suggestions, then I apologized. My approach was typically male, I told her. I honestly didn't know how a person should go about making friends. I had never done it. As a goal-oriented male, I had found that my new friends were people whom I had been working beside. We were partners in a cause, or fellow-employees, or teammates. First we were associates, then friends. My tentative advice was to sign up on a team effort to which she could consciously give herself. Along the way, she would be associated with several others among whom she could discover a potential friend.

That really wasn't bad advice, I have since decided. Friendship is often a by-product of some shared activity. Most of my friends today are those with whom I have labored in the ministry. We haven't given too much attention to our friendship; mostly we have taken it for granted. We began as associates.

Associates do not necessarily become close friends. The job or joy we share with another may, in fact, be limited only to the task or experience we have in common. Ignace Lepp made a study a few decades ago of sexual love, for example. Though it betrays a careless, though no longer uncommon, attitude about sex, the study dramatically illustrates the difficulty of achieving real intimacy in friendship. Lepp discovered that people who experienced sex together (hence, in the language of this book, thought they had found "friendship"), often remained "isolated in their solitude." They were associated in this form of physical expression, but not in the deeper communion that is love and friendship. "Finally," he writes,

> even those whose erotic love life is nearly perfect do not find it fully satisfying, for it is at best a highly fragile possession. In order to endure, it must be allied to other forms of emotional life that are less dependent upon the mutations of the flesh.[1]

Being associates in something as intimate as sexual activity is no guarantee that friendship will develop. Neither is association in marriage. Many young spouses have been disillusioned to discover that the loneliness they thought would be dispelled by marriage has instead been intensified. A formal wedding may promise a form of friendship, but it cannot guarantee the substance. Some students of the subject, in fact, have concluded that marriage and friendship are mutually exclusive. You can't have one *with* the other. Montaigne went so far as to speculate that the soul of women who marry is not strong enough to bear the weight of friendship! He had the weight of historical practice on his side. Greek men indulged in friendship with the *heraera*, those free women who were often very knowledgeable in poetry, art, and philosophy, but they would never have thought of seeking this intellectual and emotional unity with their wives. In Japan, geishas have traditionally played a similar role. We need to point out, though, that in these societies, men and women generally have not married for love.

In our society, many would-be idealists walk away from their marriages because they expect their spouses to meet them at every point of need: sexual, emotional, intellectual, social, and spiritual. They expect too much. They want their mates to be "everything" to them. Their relationships would be far healthier if they could be satisfied, in the early years of their marriage, to be associates in the common purposes of marriage and allow time for the relationship to grow naturally into a deeper communion.

Associating in any purposeful activity, then, whether in business, war, church, play, or marriage, is not the ultimate in friendship but holds the potential of developing into friendship. We make the distinction between associating and befriending because what is important in the association is not so much the persons involved as the purpose or cause to be achieved. The persons, who are never unimportant in themselves nor to be treated as mere means to an end, nonetheless subordinate themselves for the time being to the task to be accomplished.

Close Friends

Somewhere in the line of duty, you discover that one of your associates and you have a special affinity. You find yourselves laughing at the same things, grumbling about the same problems, helping each other out. The associates are on the way toward becoming close friends.

It doesn't happen with everybody—in fact, with very few—and it cannot be forced. Ignace Lepp, in his helpful book, shares a personal experience to establish his point that it takes more than being "willing" to build a good friendship. He recalls the time when he hoped to befriend a man for whom he had high respect and shared cultural, ideological, and spiritual values. He had rarely wanted so much to become anyone's friend. He confessed his desire to his associate who, apparently, had the same feelings. They both worked at it, meeting with one another, trying to do the things that make friendship possible. But it didn't work. Lepp says "the emotional spark was not forthcoming. We had to resign ourselves to being good companions, 'friends' in the broad sense of the term."[2] He warns anyone who has had a similar experience (and who hasn't?) not to consider himself incapable of friendship, but only incapable of friendship with that one person.

In spite of an occasional failure like this one, the fact remains that your associates are the ripest ground for the growing of close friendships. Some people don't take advantage of the opportunities because they consider themselves self-sufficient, or perhaps even superior to their colleagues. Still others cannot allow their companions to become friends because they have a need to dominate a relationship and control every situation. The obstacle to friendship, in other words, is in themselves, so their associates remain associates and no more.

Some famous Biblical friends have been oft maligned, but in this context I want to say a word for them. You remember the devastating trials of Job. When Eliphaz the Temanite, Bildad the Shuhite, and Zophar the Naamathite heard about all his troubles, they determined to do whatever they could to help him. Each set out from his home and, joining ranks, together they went to sympathize with and comfort their friend. Even from a distance, they could see how badly he had fallen, and they began to weep for him, tearing their robes and sprinkling dust on their heads. Then they sat beside him on the ground for seven days and seven nights, not speaking because they saw his suffering was too great for words. Only after this respectful week did their famous dialogue begin. Their words, unfortunately, were not as wise as their silence.

I call these three men more than acquaintances, even more than associates. They were indeed friends, close friends. They cared enough to suffer with him, to share his silence, and then to correct him when they feared he was wrong. Their theology was wrong, but their sympathies were admirable. They did not abandon him to his misery, but sat beside him in it.

These are men worthy of the words in Ecclesiastes 4:9-12:

> Two are better than one,
>   because they have a good return for their work:
> If one falls down,
>   his friend can help him up.
> But pity the man who falls
>   and has no one to help him up!
> Also, if two lie down together, they will keep warm.
>   But how can one keep warm alone?
> Though one may be overpowered,
>   two can defend themselves.
> A cord of three strands is not quickly broken.

The Preacher is using the language of work associates. Two working together are better than one. They produce more. One can help the other when he stumbles. Then the picture shifts. These men are more than co-workers. They are together in their off-hours. They are still working together, this time (even in their sleep) to fend off the cold. If an enemy threatens them, they fight together to defend themselves. The bond of their relationship strengthens them, so that, by joining forces, the two have the strength of three. These associates, companions, have become close friends. They may even have become intimate ones.

Intimates

Intimacy is friendship in its highest expression. The word has been perverted in our sensual age. To be intimate now commonly connotes being sexually involved, which is a misappropriation of the term. Rather, I am thinking of Jesus' remarks to His closest friends:

> I no longer call you servants, because a servant does not know his master's business. Instead, I have called you friends, for everything that I learned from my Father I have made known to you (John 15:15).

143

You know my mind, you know my heart, you know everything I can possibly share. I have held nothing back. With you my defenses are down and I am vulnerable. What I have been to my Father (the One to whom I have been the closest) you have become to Me.

Intimate. "A soul in two bodies" is Aristotle's definition of a friend. He is quick to point out that friendship implies few friends rather than many. Of acquaintances there need be no limit, and associates may be many. One may have several close friends, but of intimates (since intimacy requires proved trustworthiness over many years), we can afford only a few. Cicero finds the same likeness in friends: "In the face of a true friend a man sees as it were a second self."

An intimate friend knows one's outward life—hobbies, vocation, other relationships, passions—but also one's hidden, unseen being. A friend looks not only at the other's eyes as he talks, but he looks into and through them, seeing what a mere acquaintance or associate or even an otherwise close friend cannot see. A communion of souls is here, invisible and indecipherable to any but the communicants. Their silences are as expressive as their utterances.

This is intimacy, friendship's highest form. It is only for the mature. It eludes every attempt at manipulation; it defies all self-serving. It can never be apprehended by the person who must "do my own thing." It is forever out of reach for the perpetually childish.

As Leo Buscaglia has discovered about mature love, intimacy is impossible until we are willing to give up several destructive characteristics, especially the need . . .

to be always right.
to be first in everything.
to be constantly in control.
to be perfect.
to be loved by everyone.
to possess.
to be free of conflict and frustration.
to change others for our needs.
to manipulate.
to blame.
to dominate.[3]

A tough list, isn't it? Yet Buscaglia is correct. These are the things that block every attempt to be an intimate friend.

A tough list.

But, as the mother was trying to tell her struggling daughter, without giving up these several negative traits, the intimacy the daughter wants cannot be. They will remain mother and daughter, loving each other, but without intimate friendship.

Intimacy is for the mature.

[1]Ignace Lepp, *The Ways of Friendship* (New York: Macmillan, 1966), p. 21.
[2]Lepp, p. 37.
[3]Leo Buscaglia, *Loving Each Other* (Thorofare, NJ: Slack, 1984), pp. 197, 198.

CHAPTER THIRTEEN

What a Friend We Have in Jesus

John 15:15

For many years I was perplexed and more than a little embarrassed by Christian love talk. "Oh, how I love Jesus," the believers sing, and they speak shamelessly of their "personal relationship" with Jesus. How is it possible to be "personally related" to someone 2,000 years dead? "Oh, He's not dead. 'He lives,'" they answer in another outburst of song. "You ask me how I know He lives; He lives within my heart." But what does it mean, this living in one's heart?

Even the popular hymn we sang so often in worship compounded my confusion: "What a friend we have in Jesus." Again, how can someone I can't see, can't touch, and can't dialogue with be my friend? Besides, the song doesn't make the relationship sound as much like friendship as like abject dependency:

> All our sins and griefs to bear. . . .
> O what peace we often forfeit,
> O what needless pain we bear,
> All because we do not carry
> Everything to God in prayer.

It's a song about prayer, really, not friendship. Friends share, they do things for each other. They don't communicate by prayer.

There was that other hymn, so sentimental and meaningless to me then, yet one of the favorites of all Christians: "In the Garden." It just puzzled me; it expressed experiences completely foreign to mine. The chorus especially excluded me:

And He walks with me, and He talks with me,
And He tells me I am His own;
And the joy we share as we tarry there,
None other has ever known.

I wondered whether many people had really experienced this communion, or was it exclusively for the hyperspiritual, the emotionally super-charged? If so, I was eliminated on both counts.

Admittedly, I am a pretty emotional person; so much so, in fact, that while others have sought the Holy Spirit's help in achieving an ecstatic "high," I have relied on the Spirit to help me keep my feelings in check. But I am not a mystic. My faith did not begin with nor does it depend on any ecstatic experience, but originated in and continues because I accept the evidence about what theologians like to call the Jesus-event. I have yearned for ecstasy; I have prayed for bells and lightning and tongues and miracles, but the Lord has not dealt with me in this manner.

However, the truth of the matter is we have become friends anyway. In the course of writing this book, I have awakened with new appreciation to this profound friendship. I join in the singing with enthusiasm.

If you'll indulge me, this final chapter is an attempt to describe this peerless relationship, especially its benefits for this Christian. You must forgive the tentative, incomplete nature of my meditation here. If you were to ask me to explain any of my other friendships, I would disappoint you in that undertaking, too. All of my friends I know only partially and can explain only approximately. Human personalities and interpersonal relationships transcend the limits of human vocabulary. There's truth to that old saw, "I love my wife, but I sure can't explain her."

So I apologize for what's to follow. I'm trying to analyze the most important friendship I have, with a dear Friend I have been a long time learning to appreciate as I should. If your relationship with Him differs substantially from mine, don't think that you are out of line—or that I am. Since you and I are quite unlike one another, we must expect our friendships with Jesus to be dissimilar. We would not relate to any other friend in the same manner, either.

My Friend Jesus Keeps Me
From Thinking More Highly of Myself Than I Ought

This is the first and perhaps the best benefit of all.

A good friend is somebody who tells you the most important fact about the nature of divinity, which is that you aren't it. You may enjoy acting like God, but it's all make believe. I wouldn't have started with this benefit ordinarily, but lately I've been grieving over some young friends who are currently making themselves and everybody around them pretty miserable because they aren't prepared yet to let God be God. They keep trying to do His job. They have rejected Christianity; they have concluded that all religions are the same, hence no religion is worth getting heated up over. The final court of appeal on all decisions ethical and otherwise is their own feelings. They wouldn't admit it, but their philosophy of life is no whit different from old-fashioned Greek hedonism, even though they dress it up in designer togas.

They are not so much to be censured as pitied. As gods go, they are pretty puny ones. What they need and won't accept is a true Friend who can so capture their attention they will forget about themselves in their interest in Him. They aren't ready yet. In their search among religions, the one they won't investigate is Christianity. They are afraid they know the answer, and they aren't ready to admit they are botching their god-job.

Here is what Jesus does for us: He introduces us to the true God so we don't have to go on managing the universe ourselves. Until then, we look as ridiculous as a dog I once read about. He believed it his calling in life to help the jetliners land at the nearby airport. Whenever he heard one approaching, he began barking directions to the pilot, running back and forth the length of his backyard in an anxious frenzy until the plane had safely landed. Only then did he stop, his job completed, able to rest awhile until the next jet approached. The pilots not once expressed their gratitude to the dog for the superb job he was doing, but since he had taken on the assignment, not a single jet had crashed on approach to that airport. From their indifference, however, you'd almost have thought the pilots believed they could get along without him.

My friend Jesus has convinced me that God is competent to pilot His universe without my assistance, so I can relax and let Him be God. Jesus has done even more: He has revealed through His personality and ministry what God is like. I like what I've learned about God from my Friend. I trust Him. As George Macdonald has wisely observed, "The miracles of Jesus were the ordinary works of His Father, wrought small and swift that we might take them in."[1] In His healings, His feedings, His teachings, and His dying and rising from the dead, we behold the character and majesty of God and learn to trust His hand at the controls.

We can do more than relax; we can be honest. We don't feel the need to pretend any more. We lose our self-consciousness in our consciousness of Him. We gain a new respect for ourselves. When we play God, it's not easy to admire ourselves: we don't play the part that well. All the time we are barking orders at the airplane pilots (and anyone else we feel compelled to manage), we have a gnawing suspicion they don't take our pretensions as seriously as we do. Perhaps the plane doesn't really need our help in landing, perhaps the universe doesn't await our orders, perhaps all our manipulations and schemes are in vain.

The surprise in reciprocating Christ's desire to be our friend is that, in His company, our self-doubts, self-rejection, even sometimes self-hate disappear. This becomes very personal. Since He loves me, there must be something lovable about me. As I look to Him and forget about myself, I learn to see myself as He sees me. By forgetting myself in Him, I become more acceptable to myself. In this newfound self-confidence, I no longer need to pretend to be what I am not. I let the pilots land the planes without me.

This is a good word for our body-worshiping era, isn't it? Without a doubt, no generation in history has been more devoted to the human physique than ours. We pamper it and pump it and jog it and diet it and rearrange it through plastic surgery. We are devoted to its glory. That may be fine if you are young, tanned, lithe, and beautiful. But what if you're middle-aged, pasty, lumpy—the perfect beauty contest reject?

A real Friend doesn't love you for your packaging, but for your contents. With what relief we physical also-rans can read 1 Corinthians 6:13, "The body is not meant for sexual immorality, but for the Lord, and the Lord for the body"! When I no longer have to be God, but can offer myself in love to my loving God, I don't have to possess a perfectly divine body. It's me He loves, His Spirit seeking my Spirit, in spite of my lumps and tics.

Something more must be added about the body. Since Jesus and I have become friends, I have felt better. He has improved my health. You know how unhealthful stress is. Let me tell you, acting as your own God is the most stressful of occupations. When we turn the job back to Him, even our bodies feel the difference. As we noted in an earlier chapter, a good friend brings to us—even to our bodies—seasons of refreshing. Friendship is a tonic to tired bodies. The Best Friend is the Best Tonic of all!

My Friend Jesus Has
Given Me New Eyes With Which to See

A good friend affects your point of view. When you and a friend have seen a movie together or enjoyed a sunset or read a book, you can't wait to compare impressions. You want to know what your friend saw and thought and felt. Your points of view won't be exactly the same, so by sharing you enhance each other's experience. You see with new eyes.

Jesus affects us like this in several ways:

We Can't Look at the World Anymore Without Seeing God

The old division of everything into "sacred" and "secular" is gone. So is the separation of the spiritual (good) and the material (bad). "This is my Father's world," Jesus tells us. "Everything in it is His." If you can accept what I mean by the term, our friendship with Jesus makes us a lot more "worldly"—not in subscribing to earthbound values, not at all! But in developing a deeper appreciation of all things God-made. His natural masterpieces, His brilliant colors and splashes of light and shadow we no longer take for granted; we thank Him for it all, for He shines through it.

We Can't Look at God Without Seeing the World, Either

We remember that He so loved this world "that he gave his one and only Son" for the people in it. Because of Jesus, we can't confine worship to gazing fondly into the heavens; we look up to see Him looking down. He's watching the lost and the least. When we first fall in love with the Lord, we only have eyes for Him. As our friendship deepens, we learn to look where He looks and to love as He loves.

We Can't Look at People Without Seeing New Creatures

When you are your own god, you congratulate yourself on your superiority to the mere mortals around you. When you resign your divinity, you become far less critical of other people. His perfection makes you aware of your imperfections; His graciousness exposes your arrogance. Your perspective on humanity changes.

> So from now on we regard no one from a worldly point of view. Though we once regarded Christ in this way, we do so no longer. Therefore, if anyone is in Christ, he is a new creation; the old has gone, the new has come! (2 Corinthians 5:16-18).

You are one of those new creations. Your new eyes are endued with a compassion missing from your old nearsighted ones. This is the conclusion to which Dietrich Bonhoeffer comes:

> He stands between us and God, and for that very reason he stands between us and all other men and things. *He is the Mediator*, not only between God and man, but between man and man, between man and reality.[2]

How do these new eyes work? Let's take an extreme but true case. Several years ago, two students were assigned to be roommates in a student foundation on a university campus. There shouldn't have been a problem, since both young men were Christians. It was a grievous mistake, though, because one was *Arab* and the other *Jew*. They both believed in Christ, but they also believed in the superiority of their own cultures. When the inevitable happened, it was violent. They had to be torn apart to keep from killing each other. Finally, after days of intense counseling, they were helped to see that Christ could make them one in fact as well as in name.[3]

This is one of the toughest lessons we Christians have to learn, isn't it? A friend of His is to be a friend of mine, regardless of all the differences that distinguish us. We are now one in Christ, having been made one new person in Him (see Ephesians 2:14-18).

My Friend Jesus Has
Accepted Me in Spite of My Unacceptability

If the Bible is telling the truth—and I have no reason to disbelieve it except my own sin-driven cynicism—then I can rejoice in having a Friend who has accepted me even when He has every reason not to.

At long last, I have taken in this incredible truth: when I was still a sinner, when even I was aware of my sinfulness; even before I was willing to forgive myself for my sinfulness, my Friend embraced me. More than that, He forgave me. Romans 5:6 through 8 is for me!

> You see, at just the right time, when we were still powerless, Christ died for the ungodly. Very rarely will anyone die for a righteous man, though for a good man someone might possibly dare to die. But God demonstrates his own love for us in this: While we were still sinners, Christ died for us.

Two moments in Jesus' ministry have convinced me. The first is His baptism. John the Baptist was dipping people in the Jordan River so these penitent sinners could receive forgiveness of their sins (Luke 3:3). When Jesus came, John perceived immediately that the rite was unnecessary for Him. He had no sins to repent of. Yet Jesus insisted. He was determined to "fulfill all righteousness" (Matthew 3:15). What did that mean if not that He was thereby declaring to John, to His Father, and to all mankind His solidarity with us sinners? This is personal. There He made himself one with me, this sinner, just as, when I was baptized, I declared my solidarity with Him. He became like a sinner in this singular act so I through His grace could become like Him.

The second moment, of course, was His crucifixion, the culmination of Jesus' rescue operation for sinners. For this sinner. For me. What more could my Friend and yours do for us than lay down His life?

He didn't deceive me into thinking that it was all right I had botched up my life. He deals with us too honestly to pretend we are anything but what we are. Good friends are honest. No, He gave me eyes to see myself as I really was; then He let me know that He wanted my friendship anyway. He did all this in the most wondrous way. To keep me from being frightened away, He came in weakness. He who was strength itself became weakness so that this weak person would accept His strength.

> Who, being in very nature God,
>   did not consider equality with God something to be grasped,
> but made himself nothing,
>   taking the very nature of a servant,
>   being made in human likeness (Philippians 2:6, 7).

This He did to become my friend.

It was Philip Toynbee who pointed out that

> if God were really a wielder of mighty physical power surely he would choose for his most favoured children those who most resemble him: not the weak, the poor and the humble but the great kings of the earth. But being himself a persistent suppliant on earth it is to the weak, the humble and the supplicating that he finds it easiest to come.[4]

Toynbee is right and wrong. Jesus reveals an all-powerful God who has chosen to forsake His strength for weakness for our sake so He won't scare us away. He meets us where we are, becoming like us so that, having won our confidence, He can help us become like Him. That's true friendship, isn't it?

The fourth benefit of this friendship may not mean as much to you as it does to me:

My Friend Jesus Gives Me Something to Live for

He has signed me up as His junior partner in a Kingdom-building adventure. He is letting me help Him—me, of all people! He has given me a reason to live and made the living fun. He energizes me.

Halford Luccock has correctly observed, "Christianity is an achievement, a venture, a discovery. Its motto cannot be 'Safety first.' It must pioneer."[5] This truth may frighten some people away from this friendship with Jesus, but it has captivated me. I don't want just to exist; I want to live!

I am writing these words in a little village in remote North Central India, where Joy and I are observing the work of two pioneer missionaries, Leah Moshier and Dolly Chitwood, who left America as young women more than forty years ago to serve the Lord in this Hindu stronghold. You should hear them talk about their adventures. They have never thought of themselves as brave or extraordinary people. They are just good friends of Jesus, and they want to be with Him. Since He is concerned about some orphaned children in India, He has asked them to help Him take care of them. In the beginning, He sent them one, then another, then yet another, until they have by now taken in over 700 children (most of whom are now grown and gone). Today, they are "mothering" 200 in their crowded facility. Ask them how they manage the complex town-in-itself that is Kulpahar Kids Home, and they candidly tell you they never intended their work to grow as it has. The Lord just kept sending them unwanted children, and they couldn't let them die. The result has been a lifesaving operation that has rewarded the rescuers with a life adventurous beyond their imagining.

Dolly Chitwood and Leah Moshier (and Linda Stanton, the Arizona nurse who joined them twelve years ago) did not venture so far from home so long ago because of a devotion to some impressive abstract purpose. They just became acquainted with Jesus, got to know Him better, and heard Him when He invited them to join His ministry. They had no idea when they accepted His challenge what lay ahead of them; they didn't ask to know. Instead, they trusted Him enough to follow Him wherever. Wherever was for them a little Hindu village in a poor rural region in faraway India.

Joy and I have had the same experience, as we have already told you. If in the year we were married you had prophesied our future for us and had included only half of the adventures we have enjoyed, we'd have laughed at your fantasy. "Impossible!" we'd have told you. We knew who we were and what we were capable of. But now we aren't laughing. Instead, we're anticipating. We know the thrills aren't over. What fun we've had traveling this journey with our Friend, partners in Kingdom building!

My Friend Jesus
Dwells in My Consciousness and in My Conscience

I'm hurrying now. As I've been counting my blessings, I have listed far more than I can mention to you. Let me quickly name just a few more. The fifth benefit of my friendship with Jesus is that He lives inside me. He has come into my innermost being through His Holy Spirit. More and more, His thoughts are becoming my thoughts, His words my words, His will my will. I'm finally beginning to understand Paul's exclamation, ". . . I no longer live, but Christ lives in me. The life I live in the body, I live by faith in the Son of God, who loved me and gave himself for me" (Galatians 2:20).

When you want to think what Jesus thinks, act as Jesus acts, love as He loves, and desire what He desires, in a very real sense you can say Christ lives in you. His Spirit makes this identification with Him possible. Furthermore, the longer you are friends, the more of Him you know, because through your friendship He discloses more of himself to you, as He promised His disciples: "I have much more to say to you, more than you can now bear. But when he, the Spirit of truth, comes, he will guide you into all the truth" (John 16:12, 13).

The best human analogy of this intimate relationship is marriage. As we noted several chapters ago, we jokingly say that, after a husband and wife have lived most of their lives together, they even begin to look alike. Certainly they have in many ways learned to think alike. Listen to them for a while and you'll find them finishing each other's sentences. One of them can look across a crowded room and read what the other is thinking. They have a treasure trove of stories they love to tell on each other; they laugh and cry at the same things. They are two hearts beating each to each. He lives in her and she in him. Our intimate friendship with the Lord takes on this character.

"I no longer live, but Christ lives in me."

My Friend Jesus Is Reliable

When I am uncertain of a course of action, I ask myself what He would do. He is a sure guide.

Quite some time ago, I wrote a letter to our two youngest children, resigning as their resident conscience. They were in their late adolescent years and were increasingly restless with Dad's uninvited lectures on this or that proper course of action. I finally realized my days as their mentor were long passed. So I resigned.

It's a sobering moment, though, when you deliberately set your children free. Are they ready? Will they make wise decisions? Who will guide them? Obviously, there are many voices willing to become their consciences, most of them unworthy. What should I tell them?

As simply and sincerely as I could, I recommended Jesus. Whenever I have conscientiously asked myself what Jesus would do, and then did it, I have been safe. My worst mistakes were when I didn't consult Him, or I consulted but ignored His counsel. Of all my friends, He has given the most reliable advice. I recommended my most reliable Friend to my children. They can't go wrong heeding His counsel.

This one I must say:

I Not Only Love My Friend Jesus, but I Like Him

There's something irresistible about this complex, compelling personality that just won't let go of me. There is truth in another of those sentimental songs I couldn't understand years ago: "The longer I serve Him, the sweeter He grows." Now the song doesn't sound so sentimental. John expresses my feeling better than I can: "This is how we know what love is: Jesus Christ laid down his life for us. And we ought to lay down our lives for our brothers" (1 John 3:16). This objectively defines love. It *is* sweet to know that someone loves me with unqualified love. First, He gave himself to prove His love; that's how I know I can trust His word. He died for it. He had nothing to gain personally from it. He had no ulterior motive in doing it. It was love, pure and simple. You can understand why I eagerly love Him in return. You can't help liking someone who is so determined to save you that He'll die for you.

I Seek His Approval

I must quit, but I can't leave this confessional without mentioning this final aspect of my friendship with Jesus. I want my Friend to approve of me. It would be a much easier life for me in some ways if He weren't my friend, if I didn't care what He thinks about me. At times, I've thought about the comforts of pantheism. I could still believe in God (God is everywhere, in everything), but I wouldn't have to be committed to anything. Pantheism doesn't ask anything of me. Hedonism

157

doesn't either, except that I have a good time. Neither does atheism, since there isn't any God to care about what I do.

But being a Christian is different. The Christian faith teaches not only that God is, but that He cares about me, about what I do, about who I am becoming. He cares enough to check up on how I'm doing, whom I'm serving, and whether I'm growing. It's a bother sometimes, this having to be good for God's sake, but I'm glad He's taking notice. I'm the better for it.

My religion, you see, is more than a philosophy of life, much more than intellectual exercise or esthetic enjoyment. It's obedience to the will of One whose approval I seek, obedience that leads to more than submission.

It's reward is friendship.

¹C.S. Lewis, ed., *George Macdonald, an Anthology* (Fount Paperbacks, 1946), p. 33.

²Dietrich Bonhoeffer, *The Cost of Discipleship* (New York: Macmillan, 1937), p. 106.

³Lloyd Ogilvy tells this story in *A Life Full of Surprises* (Nashville: Abingdon, 1969), pp. 54, 55.

⁴Phillip Toynbee, *Part of a Journey* (London: William Collins & Sons, 1981), p. 206.

⁵Robert Luccock, ed., *Halford Luccock Treasury* (Nashville: Abingdon, 1963), p. 29.